全国高等教育学术英语规划系列教材

学术英语读写教程
English Reading and Writing for Academic Purposes

主　编　邹　丽
副主编　甘小亚　李　静
　　　　吴　燕　杜　峰

武汉科技大学研究生质量工程项目

苏州大学出版社

图书在版编目(CIP)数据

学术英语读写教程 = English Reading and Writing for Academic Purposes / 邹丽主编. —苏州：苏州大学出版社，2021.12(2022.9重印)
全国高等教育学术英语规划系列教材
ISBN 978-7-5672-3743-8

Ⅰ.①学… Ⅱ.①邹… Ⅲ.①英语-阅读教学-高等学校-教材②英语-写作-高等学校-教材 Ⅳ.①H319.37②H319.36

中国版本图书馆 CIP 数据核字(2021)第 208491 号

书　　名：	学术英语读写教程 English Reading and Writing for Academic Purposes
主　　编：	邹　丽
责任编辑：	王　娅
策划编辑：	汤定军
封面设计：	吴　钰
出版发行：	苏州大学出版社(Soochow University Press)
社　　址：	苏州市十梓街1号　邮编：215006
印　　装：	江苏凤凰数码印务有限公司
网　　址：	www.sudapress.com
邮　　箱：	sdcbs@suda.edu.cn
邮购热线：	0512-67480030
销售热线：	0512-67481020
开　　本：	787 mm×1 092 mm　1/16　印张：10　字数：231 千
版　　次：	2021 年 12 月第 1 版
印　　次：	2022 年 9 月第 2 次印刷
书　　号：	ISBN 978-7-5672-3743-8
定　　价：	48.00 元

凡购本社图书发现印装错误，请与本社联系调换。服务热线：0512-67481020

PREFACE

This textbook is intended for English for general academic purposes. It uses authentic content to provide both the basic concepts of English for academic purposes and the reading and writing skills necessary for academic purposes.

The book consists of three units. All the units will expose you to some frequently used academic conventions and provide various practice to help you to develop essential skills in English reading and writing for academic purposes.

Unit 1 is a preparatory part. It includes

◇ how to read the copyright page of an academic book and the title page of a journal paper;

◇ how to use a dictionary to learn when and where to use a specific word (register);

◇ how to use proper registers in writing or oral settings;

◇ what academic words are;

◇ how to write grammatically correct sentences and read long sentences.

Unit 2 is organized by the modes of discourse: narration, description, exposition and argument. They are the basic elements of various texts. This part exposes you to some typical language phenomena in academic English and provides some basic training in narrating, describing, exposing and arguing:

◇ view points of narration, persons in journal papers, reporting skills and reporting words;

◇ senses and description, objective description in academic settings, wording in description;

◇ forms of exposition, expository devices;

◇ moves in journal papers and hedging strategies in argument.

Supplementary readings in this part are authentic texts in EAP and EST

(English for science and technology). They give you more chances of observing the language phenomena and skills discussed in each lesson and provide extra practice.

Unit 3 dedicates to academic communication in international conference settings. It brings into consideration the needs of novice writers who feel both fresh and frustrated when preparing for academic conferences and international publishing. This part involves both reading and writing communication, from inquiring about conference activities to corresponding with conference organizers and paper reviewers at different stages:

◇ how to read "call for the paper";

◇ how to inquire about conference activities;

◇ how to confirm attendance;

◇ how to correspond with paper reviewers or editors.

Disciplinary-related activities and tasks we designed through out the course, especially those in the **Project** part will encourage you to strengthen the bond between English language learning and English using in your real academic study and research practice. Putting English learning in academic-specific contexts has always been the goal of building this book.

We hope you enjoy using *English Reading and Writing for Academic Purposes*.

ZOU Li

CONTENTS

- **Unit 1 Starting up** / 1
    - Lesson 1   Reading from the beginning   / 2
    - Lesson 2   Style guides   / 10
    - Lesson 3   Style, register and dictionary use   / 19
    - Lesson 4   Sentence basics   / 29
- **Unit 2 Modes of discourse** / 40
    - Lesson 1   Narration (1)   / 41
    - Lesson 2   Narration (2)   / 50
    - Lesson 3   Description (1)   / 58
    - Lesson 4   Description (2)   / 66
    - Lesson 5   Exposition   / 76
    - Lesson 6   Argument (1)   / 92
    - Lesson 7   Argument (2)   / 103
    - Lesson 8   Journal paper reading   / 110
- **Unit 3 Academic communication** / 121
    - Lesson 1   "Call for papers" announcement   / 122
    - Lesson 2   Conference correspondence   / 133
- **Appendixes** / 143
- **References** / 150

English Reading and Writing for Academic Purposes

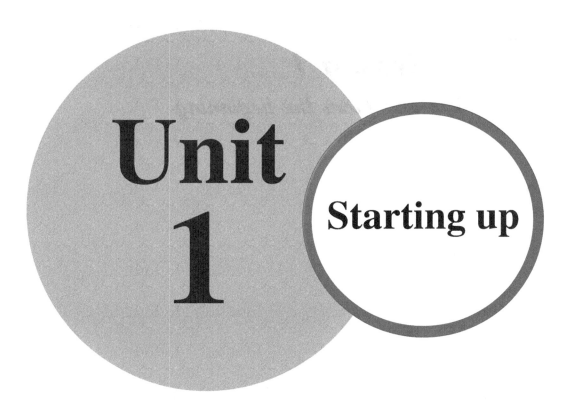

Lesson 1
Reading from the beginning

Overview

☑ Listening
- Copyright page words

☑ Reading
- The copyright page
- The title page

☑ Translation
- Names

☑ Project
- Talking about the corresponding author and the first author

☑ Further reading & references

Listening

Dictation.

1. _____ is where a reader would find out who owns the copyright for a specific book.
2. The copyright page often locates in the front of a book that lists publication, notice, copyright, printing, _____ and _____ information.
3. ISBN stands for _____.
4. _____ is a person who prepares a final copy of something by taking out extra words and fixing errors.
5. _____ is a version of something, or a style in which a book is printed.
6. All libraries need to manage and _____ their books to be able to keep track of their stock as well as determine what books have been checked out.
7. Bookbinding styles range from simple to more complicated. You can tape your book, _____ it with a ribbon, or even sew it in place.
8. When writing a research paper, finding and citing appropriate sources are the most important aspects of backing up your thesis. Proper sourcing or giving _____ to sources can contribute to strong arguments in your paper.

Reading: The copyright page

❶ **Discuss the following questions with your classmates.**

1. Have you ever noticed the copyright page of a book or a magazine?
   _____

2. Where do you think the copyright page is located in a book?
   _____

3. What elements can you find in the copyright page?
   _____

4. Who cares about what kind of information presented on the copyright page?
   _____

1) Librarians	a. to know how to use quotations from the book
2) Authors	b. to retrieve the book information
3) Publishers	c. whose works are protected as intellectual property
4) Bookstores and wholesalers	d. to claim the ownership of their original work
5) Readers	e. to know how to contact the publisher
	f. to credit those who contribute to the work

❷ **Read the introduction to the copyright page and check your answers in ❶.**

Copyright page

A copyright page is usually the verso of the title page. This page usually carries the following elements: copyright notice, edition information, publication information, printing history, cataloging data, legal notices, and the book's ISBN or identification number. In addition, rows of numbers are sometimes printed at the bottom of the page to indicate the year and the number of the printing. Credits for design, production, editing and illustration are also commonly listed on the copyright page.

❸ **Read the following copyright page and identify the elements it contains.**

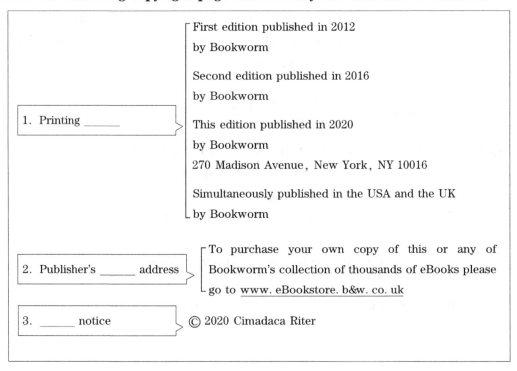

continued

4. _____ notice	All rights reserved. No part of this book may be reprinted or reproduced or utilized in any form or by any electric, mechanical or other means, now known or hereafter invented, including photocopying and recording, or in any information storage of retrieval system, without permission in writing from the publishers. For permissions contact: ask@ Bookworm. com
5. _____ for design	Cover by John Weber
6. Country and printing	Printed and bound in the UK

7. _____ data	Ebook ISBN: 987-0-415-76825-1
	British Library of Congress Cataloging-in-Publication Data
	  Riter, Cimadaca, 1960 –
	    Academic English: From Reading to Writing
	    Cimadaca Riter. – 1st ed.
	Includes bibliographical references and index.
	1. Academic reading. 2. Academic writing. 3. Cross discipline

8. _____	ISBN13: 987-0-415-57310-2 (hbk) ISBN13: 987-0-415-57311-6 (pbk) ISBN13: 987-0-415-76825-1 (ebk)

❹ **Read the above copyright page carefully and answer the questions below.**

1. What is the title of the book?

   _____

2. Who is the author?

   _____

3. What is the edition of this book?

   _____

4. When and where was it published?

   _____

5. What is the ISBN of the hardcover edition of the book?

❺ **Read the copyright pages of two textbooks in your field and complete the following table with the copyright page information of the books.**

Your major		
Copyright page elements	Book 1	Book 2
Book title		
Author(s)		
Edition		
Publishing time & place		
ISBN		
How would you cite the books in MLA citation style in the bibliography of your term paper?*		

(*Note: To answer this question, please refer to MLA citation style <https://owl.purdue.edu/owl/research_and_citation/mla_style/mla_formatting_and_style_guide/mla_formatting_and_style_guide.html> to learn how to cite a book in MLA style in your academic paper.)

Reading: The title page

❶ **Read the title page of a journal paper and answer the following questions.**

1. What is the journal?

2. What is the title of the paper? When was the paper published? In which volume is it published? How many pages does it have?

3. Who are the authors?

4. Who will first get the reviews back from the journal and have the experience of preparing a response to the editor of the journal? Why?

5. Why is the title page information important?

The title page of a journal paper:

Chemical Geology 453 (2017) 72–79

Contents lists available at ScienceDirect

Chemical Geology

journal homepage: www.elsevier.com/locate/chemgeo

Immobilization of nanoparticles by occlusion into microbial calcite

Rebecca L. Skuce [a], Dominique J. Tobler [a,b], Ian MacLaren [c], Martin R. Lee [a], Vernon R. Phoenix [d],*

[a] School of Geographical & Earth Sciences, Gregory Building, University of Glasgow, G12 8QQ, UK
[b] Nano-Science Center, Department of Chemistry, University of Copenhagen, Universitetsparken 5, 2100 Copenhagen Ø, Denmark
[c] School of Physics and Astronomy, University of Glasgow, G12 8QQ, UK
[d] Department of Civil and Environmental Engineering, University of Strathclyde, Glasgow, G1 1XJ, UK

ARTICLE INFO

Article history:
Received 6 December 2016
Received in revised form 3 February 2017
Accepted 4 February 2017
Available online 6 February 2017

Keywords:
Calcite
Occlusion
Nanoparticle
Bacteria
Ureolysis
Biomineralization

ABSTRACT

Binding of nanoparticles (NPs) to mineral surfaces influences their transport through the environment. The potential, however, for growing minerals to immobilize NPs via occlusion (the process of trapping particles inside the growing mineral) has yet to be explored in environmentally relevant systems. In this study, the ureolytic bacteria *Sporosarcina pasteurii* was used to induce calcium carbonate precipitation in the presence of organo-metallic manufactured nanoparticles. As calcite crystals grew the nanoparticles in the solution became trapped inside these crystals. Capture of NPs within the calcite via occlusion was verified by transmission electron microscopy of thin foils. Nanoparticles with a negative surface charge were captured with greater efficiency than those with a positive surface charge, resulting from stronger attachment of negative nanoparticles to the positively charged calcite surfaces, which in turn facilitated occlusion. Thermodynamic and kinetic analysis, however, did not reveal a significant difference in k_p (calcite precipitation rate constant) or the critical saturation at which precipitation initiates (S_{crit}), indicating the presence of different charged nanoparticles did not influence calcite precipitation at the concentrations used here. Overall, these findings demonstrate that microbially driven mineral precipitation has potential to immobilize nanoparticles in the environment via occlusion.

© 2017 The Authors. Published by Elsevier B.V. This is an open access article under the CC BY license (http://creativecommons.org/licenses/by/4.0/).

1. Introduction

Microorganisms have the ability to drive the precipitation of a wide range of minerals. This process can lead to the immobilization of dissolved metals, either within the crystalline structure of the mineral or bound to the mineral surface. For example, microbial oxidation of Fe(II) and Mn(II) generates metal (hydr)oxides which can absorb various dissolved heavy metals and metalloids (Martinez et al., 2004; Pei et al., 2013), while enzymatic precipitation of phosphate produces hydroxyapatite which binds significant quantities of dissolved heavy metals (Handley-Sidhu et al., 2011). Calcite precipitation is common in ground and surface water systems and can be abiotically or biotically driven. A variety of microbial pathways can drive calcite precipitation, including photosynthesis (Merz, 1992), denitrification (van Paassen et al., 2010) and sulphate reduction (Braissant et al., 2007). The capacity to hydrolyse urea (ureolysis) is common in soil and aquifer microorganisms and also has the ability to drive calcite precipitation (Fujita et al., 2010). This process can be manipulated for solid phase capture of heavy metals and radionuclides, where the foreign ion gets incorporated into the calcium carbonate crystal structure as it forms (e.g., ^{90}Sr replacing Ca in the crystal lattice), thus preventing their mobility in the subsurface (Warren et al., 2001). During ureolysis-driven calcium carbonate precipitation, urea is hydrolysed by the microbial enzyme urease, producing ammonia and carbonic acid (Eq. (1)), which then equilibrates in water to form bicarbonate, ammonium and hydroxide ions. This leads to a pH rise and if soluble calcium is present, an increase in $CaCO_3$ saturation state. Once $CaCO_3$ becomes supersaturated, $CaCO_3$ minerals such as calcite precipitate (Tobler et al., 2011) (Eq. (2)).

$$CO(NH_2)_2 + 2H_2O \rightleftharpoons 2NH_3 + H_2CO_3 \quad (1)$$

$$Ca^{2+} + HCO_3^- \rightleftharpoons CaCO_3 + H^+ \quad (2)$$

While solid phase capture of dissolved metals during microbial mineral precipitation is a well-known and studied process, the fate of nanometre sized particles during microbial mineral precipitation has not been examined in detail. With a rising demand for nanomaterials and continual growth in production, increased environmental exposure to manufactured nanoparticles (NPs) is likely (Caballero-Guzman and Nowack, 2016). NPs also occur naturally, and both manufactured and natural NPs can act as carriers of heavy metals and organic contaminants (Hofmann and von der Kammer, 2009). To date, investigations into the impact of minerals on nanoparticle transport and fate in the natural environment have largely focused upon the adhesion of

* Corresponding author.
E-mail address: vernon.phoenix@strath.ac.uk (V.R. Phoenix).

http://dx.doi.org/10.1016/j.chemgeo.2017.02.005
0009-2541/© 2017 The Authors. Published by Elsevier B.V. This is an open access article under the CC BY license (http://creativecommons.org/licenses/by/4.0/).

❷ **Find two latest/classic journal articles in your field. Read their title pages and complete the following table with their title page information.**

Your major		
Information	Paper 1	Paper 2
Title of the journal		
Volume		
Title of the paper		
Author(s)		
Corresponding author		
Publishing time		
Page		
How would you cite the papers in MLA citation style in the bibliography of your term paper?*		

(*Note: Still, please refer to MLA citation style <https://owl.purdue.edu/owl/research_and_citation/mla_style/mla_formatting_and_style_guide/mla_formatting_and_style_guide.html> to learn how to cite a paper in MLA style in your academic paper.)

Translation

Who are these people in the following table? What are their names in Chinese/English?

English name	Chinese name	Description
	屠呦呦	The first Chinese Nobel winner in physiology or medicine who discovered artemisinin（青蒿素）used to treat malaria.
	司马迁	
Stephen Hawking		
	薛定谔	
	王尔德	
	汤若望	
Matteo Ricci		
	马伯乐	
John King Fairbank		
	史景迁	

	continued	
English name	**Chinese name**	**Description**
the Wright brothers		
	李政道	
	丁肇中	
	(你的名字)*	

* Note: Do you have an English name? If you have, please write it in the corresponding column.

Project

- What is the corresponding author?
- What is the first author?
- And what are the differences between the corresponding author and the first author?

Use resource materials, such as the Internet or an encyclopedia, and discuss the above questions with your partners. Work out a short report based on your findings and bring it to the next class.

Further reading & references

- 新华通讯社译名室.《世界人名翻译大辞典》.中译出版社(原中国对外翻译出版公司). 2007.
  附录: · 世界各国及地区语言、民族、宗教和人名翻译主要依据
  · 威妥玛式拼法与汉语拼音对照表
  · 常用姓名后缀
  · 部分国家(民族)姓名简介

Lesson 2
Style guides

Overview

☑ **Discussion**

- The titles of books, magazines, newspapers, essays, etc.

☑ **Reading**

- Popular style guides
- Style in graphics
- Style in titles

☑ **Project**

- Talking about the citation requirements from journals

☑ **Further reading & references**

Discussion

❶ Have you noticed how the titles of books, magazines, newspapers, essays are composed and formatted? Discuss the following question with your classmates: What are the conventions of writing a proper academic essay title?

❷ Judge if the following statements are true(T) or false(F).
1. (   ) The title of a book should be presented inside quotation marks.
2. (   ) You can also underline a book title to tell your readers it is a book.
3. (   ) When writing the title of a book in English, italicize it.
4. (   ) There is no need to put quotation marks around indented passages. The only time indented passages have quotation marks is when you're citing dialogues.

Reading: Popular style guides

❶ Read the following introduction to the popular style guides in the world.

What Is a Style Guide and Which One Do You Need?

A style guide is a set of editing and formatting standards for use by students, researchers, journalists, and other writers.

Also known as style manuals, stylebooks, and documentation guides, style guides are essential reference works for writers seeking publication, especially those who need to document their sources in footnotes, endnotes, parenthetical citations, and/or bibliographies.

These manuals promote proper grammar and ensure consistency in areas where grammar is unclear. Style guides answer all those burly writing questions that are absent from the rules of grammar: Do you use a serial comma in the first paragraph, but leave it out in the third? Do you use italics in one post to refer to a book title, but in another post use quotation marks?

Basically, a style guide is an all-purpose writing resource.

Different fields, workplaces and publishers have their own preferred styles of writing.

APA Publication Manual

Foreword, *APA Publication Manual*

"From its inception as a brief journal article in 1929, the 'Publication Manual of the American Psychological Association' has been designed to advance scholarship by setting sound and rigorous standards for scientific communication."

"The *Publication Manual* is consulted not only by psychologists but also by students and researchers in education, social work, nursing, business, and many other behavioral and social sciences."

Guardian Style (UK)

Introduction, "Guardian Style"

"[T]o say that journalists are 'required' to read the stylebook may suggest that it could be considered a bit of a chore. Hardly. For a great many of us ... it is exciting and necessary stuff, moving enough to have had us reaching for a pen or hastening to our keyboard, perhaps in an initial letter."

MLA Handbook

J. Gibaldi, "*MLA Handbook* for writers of research papers"

"MLA style represents a consensus among teachers, scholars, and librarians in the fields of language and literature on the conventions for documenting research, and those conventions will help you organize your research paper coherently."

Turabian (Chicago Style)

Preface, *A Manual for Writers of Research Papers, Theses, and Dissertations: Chicago Style for Students and Researchers* "[*A Manual for Writers of Research Papers, Theses, and Dissertations*] has been extensively revised to follow the recommendations in *The Chicago Manual of Style*, 15th edition (2003), to incorporate current technology as it affects all aspects of student writing."

Which Style Guide to Use?

Very often, a style guide is not only appropriate, it is mandatory. And many disciplines have their own style guides. Most newspapers adhere to *The Associated Press Stylebook on Briefing on Media Law* (often called *The AP Stylebook*), whereas a small press publisher might ask you to use *The Elements of Style* (often referred to as "Strunk and White"). Professors and teachers generally require students to use the *MLA Handbook for Writers of Research Papers*, sixth edition.

In many cases, the matter of which style guide to use is not up to the writer. Publishers will provide guidelines explaining which style guide is required.

If technical and academic writers are writing for submission, it is a good idea to check a publication's submission guidelines to see if they require writers to use a particular style guide.

❷ **Judge if the following statements are true(T) or false(F).**

1. (　　) A style guide establishes rules for both language (including grammar and punctuation) and formatting.

2. (　　) The purpose of using a style guide is to maintain consistency when writing.

3. (　　) Within academia, style guides provide standards for citations, references, and bibliographies.
4. (　　) Different disciplines have their own style guides, such as the *Publication Manual of the American Psychological Association.*
5. (　　) A psychological major preparing a journal paper should refer to APA Style for formatting.
6. (　　) Chicago Style is popular in the fields of language and literature.
7. (　　) Chicago Style is an abbreviated version of Chicago Manual of Style.
8. (　　) All the style guides are universally used.
9. (　　) The Economist Style Guide and Guardian Style are conventional style guides in Britain.

Reading: Style in graphics

Different contexts and readership call for different styles. The four charts or pictures presented below are from different backgrounds and media and hence for different readership:

(1) A report from a technology research and an advisory company
(2) An academic paper from an international journal
(3) A user manual
(4) A newspaper report

Compare their differences. Guess their sources and readership and explain why.

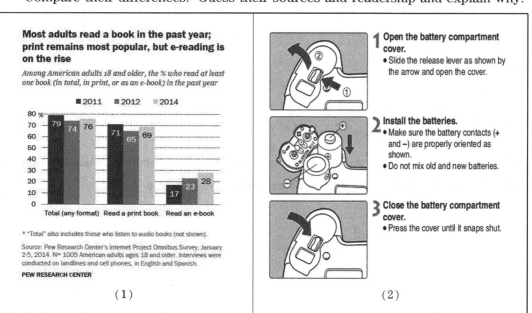

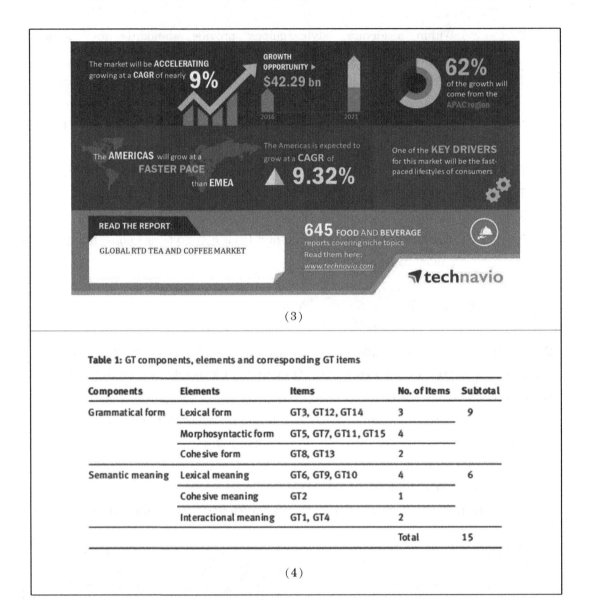

(3)

(4)

Reading: Style in titles

❶ Read the following passage introducing how to format titles in different situations. Complete the notes after the passage while reading.

Formatting Titles: Italics, Underline, Quotation Marks—Oh My!

In academic writing, authors occasionally need to refer to previously published works. However, given the myriad of formatting techniques used to highlight the titles of these works, such as italics, underlining, and quotation marks, new authors can easily become confused with the proper way to format these titles. Thankfully, the rules are not terribly difficult, and one quick question to yourself can help you sort out the proper formatting quickly.

The titles of stand-alone published works (e.g. books, journals, newspapers, albums, or movies) should be italicized. Simply ask yourself if the work appears as an independent, stand-alone volume. If the answer is yes, then the title should be italicized. For example, a newspaper title should be italicized (e.g. *The Washington Post*). Also, the title of a book should be italicized (e.g. *Little Women* by Louisa May Alcott).

At this point, I should mention underlining. Historically, underlining was used almost interchangeably with italics for the titles of these stand-alone works. This was once considered an acceptable treatment of titles because the average person did not have access to the typewriters that were required to produce italicized words. This is especially true of handwritten documents. However, with the advent of word processors, personal computers, and printers, most people can now easily produce italicized text. Thus, underlining has fallen out of favor with exception to handwritten text.

The titles of portions of a larger text or work (e.g. a chapter in a book, an article in a journal or newspaper, an individual song on an album, or a scene in a movie) should appear enclosed in quotation marks. Simply ask yourself if the work appears as part of a larger work. If the answer is yes, then enclose the title in quotation marks. For example, the article entitled "FBI Agents Finds Nixon Aides Sabotaged Democrats" as published in *The Washington Post* or the chapter "Playing Pilgrims" in *Little Women* should be handled in this way.

This little question will help you effectively format titles in most situations. However, I would be remiss if I did not mention the few unusual situations. For example, works of art (e.g. the name of a painting) should always be italicized.

The specific names of ships, planes, and spacecrafts should be italicized, but the abbreviations before the names, designations of classes, and the makes are not italicized (e.g. The *Queen Mary*, USS *Indianapolis*, Boeing 747, and The Space Shuttle *Challenger*).

The names of trains are not italicized. Also, the general names of standard religious texts use no special formatting beyond capitalization (e.g. the Bible, the Talmud, and the Koran).

Notes: How to format titles

Introduction

1. Daunting experience for new authors
   Reason: _____
2. Some techniques to highlight titles
   - ☐ Italicizing
   - ☐ Underlining
   - ☐ _____

Specific techniques

1. Italicizing
   - ☐ _____ published works
   - ☐ Books
   - ☐ _____
   - ☐ Newspapers
   - ☐ _____
   - ☐ _____

2. Underlining
   - In the past: Underlining = _____ (titles of stand-alone works).
     Reason: Not all people have the typewriters that can produce italicized words. Especially in _____ situation.
   - Technology development:
     Word processors
     _____
     Printers

3. Quotation marks
   Enclose in quotation marks the titles of _____ of a larger text
   - ☐ A _____ in a book
   - ☐ An _____ in a _____ /newspaper
   - ☐ An individual _____ on an album
   - ☐ A _____ in a movie

   Exceptions: Italicize the following
   - ☐ Works of art: The name of a _____
   - ☐ Names of _____, _____, and _____

   → Exceptions: (no italicizing)
   - ☐ _____ before the names
   - ☐ Designations of _____
   - ☐ Makes
   - ☐ Names of _____
   - ☐ General names of standard _____ texts

❷ **Notice how the following titles and sentences are edited and formatted. Improve the poor editing or formatting.**

1. Domestic animated blockbuster Ne Zha to sail overseas (*a news report title)
2. Nonlinear aging of cylindrical Lithium-ion cells linked to heterogeneous compression (*a journal article tittle)
3. Journal of energy Storage (*a journal tittle)
4. Translation of Addressing in 《Hong Lou Meng》 (*a journal paper tittle)
5. "Human security" and "environmental human rights": a review of "Human security and the UN: a Critical History" (a translation of an academic paper title: "人的安全"与"环境人权"——兼评《人的安全和联合国:一部批判史》)
6. Bi Sheng's invention was recorded by Shen Kuo (1031 – 1095), the Chinese polymath, scientist and statesman, in his book The Dream Pool Essays in 1088 AD.
7. The second season of "Flavorful Origins", another masterpiece by Chinese food documentary director Chen Xiaoqing, the creator of "A bite of China", will premiere on Sept. 9 on Tencent.com.
8. *Fuxing*, also known as *Rejuvenation*, represents China's self-developed new-generation bullet trains.
9. The exhibition *Prosperity in Tranquility: The Art of Qi Baishi* was presented at the Forbidden City in the galleries of the main tower and western wing tower at the Meridian Gate (*Wu men*) in July, 2018.

❸ **Read the following items of references. Pay close attention to how the book titles, journal titles and article titles are formatted. Try to identify them.**

1. Luke, A. (2000). Critical literacy in Australia: A matter of context and standpoint. *Journal of Adolescent & Adult Literacy*, 43 (5), 448–461.
2. Chapelle, C. (Ed.). (2000). *Computers Applications in Second Language Acquisition*. Cambridge: Cambridge University Press.
3. Cohen, L. & Manion, L. (Eds.). (1994). *Research Methods in Education*. London: Routledge.
4. Collins, B. & Wende, M. (2002). *Models of Technology and Change in Higher Education: An International Comparative Survey on the Current and Future Use of ICT in Higher Education*. Center for Higher Education Policy studies. Available: http://www.utwente.nl/cheps/documenten/ictrapport.pdf.
5. Jarvis, H. (2001). Internet usage of English for academic purposes courses.

ReCALL, 13/2, 206-212.

6. Sharma, P. (1998). *CD-ROM: A Teacher's Handbook*. Oxford: Summertown.

❹ Find two textbooks and two journal articles in your field and work out a short reference list in the format of the above examples in ❸. Translate the titles and publishing houses into English if the textbooks are written in Chinese.

1. _____.
2. _____.
3. _____.
4. _____.

Project

1. Choose two academic journals in your field and discuss with your classmates how and where to check out the citation requirements from journals. Be prepared to report your findings to the class.

2. Read "Read APA Format: 12 Basic Rules" (https://www.verywellmind.com/general-rules-for-apa-format-2794840) and "How to Reference Journal Articles in APA Format" (https://www.verywellmind.com/how-to-reference-articles-in-apa-format-2794849). Create references for at least four classic journal articles in your own field.

Further reading & references

1. American Psychological Association: https://www.apa.org/index.
2. MLA Style Center: https://style.mla.org/.
3. The Chicago Manual of Style Online: https://www.chicagomanualofstyle.org/tools_citationguide.html.

Lesson 3
Style, register and dictionary use

Overview

☑ Reading
- A story
- Wording and style
- Register

☑ Drilling
- Style & wording
- Academic words & dictionary using

☑ Vocabulary

☑ Project

Reading

❶ Do you know the following words? Try to explain them with your own words.

1. a perforation	a hole
2. a base	
3. an apex	
4. an aperture	
5. to inhale	
6. to discharge	
7. contents	
8. to exclaim	
9. a gal	
10. to suck	

❷ Read the following story and answer the questions after it.

> A young lady back home from school was explaining. "Take an egg," she said, "and make a perforation in the base and a corresponding one in the apex, then apply the lips to the aperture, and by forcibly inhaling the breath, the shell is entirely discharged of its contents."
>
> An old lady who was listening exclaimed, "It beats all how folks do things nowadays. When I was a gal, they made a hole in each end and sucked."

1. What is the effect of the story? The story is _____.
   A. serious   B. humorous   C. ironic   D. instructive
2. What makes the story achieve such an effect?

_____

❸ Look up the words in ❶ (also the key words in the story) in the following online dictionaries. Fill in the table with their definitions, and compare the definitions of each word.

1. *Longman Dictionary of Contemporary English Online*: https://www.ldoceonline.com/.
2. *Oxford Dictionary*: https://www.oxfordlearnersdictionaries.com/.
3. *Cambridge Dictionary*: https://dictionary.cambridge.org/.
4. *Youdao Dictionary*: http://dict.youdao.com/.

	Longman	*Oxford*	*Cambridge*	*Youdao*
1. a perforation				
2. a base				
3. an apex				
4. an aperture				
5. to inhale				
6. to discharge				
7. contents				
8. to exclaim				
9. a gal				
10. to suck				

❹ **Read the entries of the words you have consulted. Compare the entries of "perforation" from five (e)dictionaries, identify their components and fill in the last roll ("Component") with the help of the following items that frequent a dictionary.**

parts of speech	phonetic	pronunciation
etymology/origin	collocation	plural form of a noun
register	definition in English	example of use
synonym	antonym	translation

Dictionary	Entry	Component
LONGMAN	**per · fo · ra · tion** *formal* **1** [countable usually plural] a small hole in something, especially one of a line of holes made in a piece of paper so that it can be torn easily: ◀) *the perforations in a sheet of stamps*	1. syllables 2. register 3. _____ 4. _____ 5. _____
Oxford Learner's Dictionaries	**perforation** *noun* BrE /ˌpɜːfəˈreɪʃn/ ◀); NAmE /ˌpɜːrfəˈreɪʃn/ ◀) 1 ★ [countable, usually plural] a small hole in a surface, often one of a series of small holes • *Tear the sheet of stamps along the perforations.* • *He made a small perforation in the lining of the tube.* 2 ★ [uncountable] (*medical*) the process of splitting or tearing in such a way that a hole is left • *Excessive pressure can lead to perforation of the stomach wall.* ➕ Word Origin	1. _____ 2. _____ 3. _____ 4. _____ 5. _____ 6. _____

continued

Dictionary	Entry	Component
Cambridge Dictionary	**perforation** noun • UK /ˌpɜːrˈfeɪ.ʃən/ US /ˈpɜː.fəˈreɪ.ʃən/ [C] a hole in something: A tea bag is full of tiny perforations. [C or U] medical SPECIALIZED a hole that goes all the way through a membrane or tissue or the act of making a hole like this: One possible complication of colonoscopy is a perforation through the bowel wall that could require surgery. —Thesaurus: synonyms and related words Holes, hollows and dips	1. _____ 2. _____ 3. _____ 4. _____ 5. _____ 6. _____ 7. _____
有道 youdao	**perforation** 英 [ˌpɜːfəˈreɪʃn] 美 [ˌpɜːrfəˈreɪʃn] n. 穿孔；贯穿 [复数 perforations]	1. _____ 2. _____ 3. _____ 4. _____
金山词霸	基础知识 / 基础释义 / 双语例句 / 权威解析 / 柯林斯 / 牛津词典 / 英汉双解 / 词汇扩展 / 行业词典 / 划译 **perforation** 英 [pɜːfəˈreɪʃn] 美 [pɜrfəˈreɪʃn] n. 穿孔；贯穿；针孔；齿孔 变形 复数： perforations 双语例句 1.The acute perforation has developed. 发生急性穿孔。 2.Involvement of the small bowel by primary or metastic neoplasms may occasionally be followed by perforation. 原发性或转移性肿瘤累及小肠也偶可继发穿孔。	1. _____ 2. _____ 3. _____ 4. _____ 5. _____

❺ **Compare the registers of the following words in *Longman Dictionary of Contemporary English*.**

	Register		Register
1. a perforation	formal, technical	2. an apex	
an aperture		a top	
a hole			
3. to inhale		4. to exclaim	
to suck		to shout	
5. a gal			
a maiden			

❻ **Keep in mind the registers of the words you consulted and read the story again. After the second reading, answer the following questions.**

1. What are the differences of the following synonyms *perforation*, *aperture*, *hole*; *apex base*, *end*; *inhale the breath*, *suck* in terms of **meaning** and **situation** (e.g. when and where) where they are usually used? Which part of the dictionary entries tell you this?

   _____
   _____

2. What is the likely relationship between the young lady and the old lady? Where are they? When do they have this dialogue? How do they choose words?

   _____

3. Have you had a new interpretation of the story? What makes this change? What kind of information in dictionary entries do you find helpful in interpreting the story?

   _____
   _____

4. Besides definition, which items from the dictionary entries can help you choose a proper word from many similar words?

   _____

Drilling

❶ **Compare and analyze the language features of the following two pairs of passages. Compare your analysis with your classmates' and discuss the questions after the passages.**

Pair 1

Passage A

In climatology, spring is the season of the year between winter and summer during which temperatures gradually rise. It is generally defined in the Northern Hemisphere as extending from the vernal equinox (day and night equal in length), march 20 or 21, to the summer solstice (year's longest day), June 21 or 22, and in the Southern Hemisphere from September 22 or 23 to December 22 or 23 ...

Passage B

Springs are not always the same. In some years, April bursts upon our Virginia hills in one prodigious leap—and all the stage is filled at once, whole choruses of tulips, arabesques of forsythia, cadenzas of flowering plum. The trees grow leaves overnight.

In other years, spring tiptoes in. It pauses, overcome by shyness, like my grandchild at the door, peeping in, ducking out of sight, giggling in the hallway. "I know you're out there," I cry. "Come in!" and April slips into our arms.

1. In terms of writing style, which passage is formal and which is informal? And what makes them formal or informal?
2. Who might be the writers and readers of these two passages?
3. Passage A is likely to be from _____; and Passage B is likely to be from _____.

    (1) a literature magazine
    (2) an encyclopedia

Pair 2

Passage A

People get natural rubber from rubber trees as a white, milky liquid, which is called latex. They mix it with acid, and dry it, and then they sent it to countries all over the world. As the rubber industry grew, people needed more and more rubber. They started rubber plantations in countries with hot, wet weather conditions, but these still could not give enough raw rubber to meet the needs of growing industry.

Passage B

Natural rubber is obtained from rubber trees as a white, milky liquid known as latex. This is treated with acid and dried before being dispatched to countries all over the world. As the rubber industry developed, more and more rubber was required. Rubber plantations were established in countries with a hot, humid climate, but these still could not supply sufficient raw rubber to satisfy the requirements of developing industry.

1. Compare the style of the two passages by completing the following tasks. The table after the tasks may help you analyze their features.

(1) There are many pairs of synonyms in the two passages. Compare their meanings and styles (oral or written, formal or informal) by consulting *Longman Dictionary of Contemporary English Online*.

(2) Compare the sentence features of the two passages.

		Passage A			Passage B	
		Meaning	Register (Formal/ Informal)		Meaning	Register (Formal/ Informal)
Wording	get			obtain		
	sent			dispatch		
	grew			develop		
	start			establish		
	meet the needs			satisfy the requirements		
(Summary)						
Sentence	Passive voice					
	Active voice					
(Summary)						

2. Passage A is _____ and fit for _____; and Passage B is _____ and proper for _____.

   A. formal

   B. informal

   C. a lecture intended for middle school students

   D. a pop science magazine

❷ **Judge whether the following sentences are formal or informal. Tick (√) the correct brackets.**

Formal	Informal	
( )	( )	1. There's one big problem.
( )	( )	2. However, there are serious drawbacks to this approach which relies very much on the analyst's interpretation skills and subjective judgement.

continued

Formal	Informal	
( )	( )	3. Nuclear power is relatively cheap. On the other hand, you could argue that it's not safe.
( )	( )	4. The whales aren't confusing sonar with killer whale sounds likely because it is loud.
( )	( )	5. They've come across a few problems that need resolving.
( )	( )	6. The team of researchers had encountered similar problems before.
( )	( )	7. If customer complaints don't come your way, go down to the Customer Relations Department and chat to the people there.
( )	( )	8. If a 30 to 40-ton animal falls, it's going to be dead.

❸ **Rewrite the following sentences to make them formal.**

Example: Another thing to think about is the chance of crime getting worse.

→*Another aspect to consider is the possibility of crime deteriorating.*

1. Today, public tolerance of slang is at an all-time high—just look at how widely it's used in newspapers.

2. Working memory, the second type of memory, allows us to hold on to things for as long as we think about them.

3. Kids in America today watch about 1,500 hours of TV every day. Compare that to the amount of time that they spend in school each year, about 900 hours, and you can see that TV must have a big impact.

4. I'll talk about three common types of modern art: pop art, realism, and surrealism.

5. There are other more important things for getting happiness.

6. We analyzed the data and we found that there are more and more human noises (shipping, military sonar, seismic air guns, and construction).

7. To tell apart small plant parts such as reproductive structures, people need a hand lens or a low magnification microscope for close checking.

Vocabulary

❶ The four pairs of similar words in the following box are ACADEMIC WORDS, which are frequently used in academic settings. Looking them up in *Longman Dictionary of Contemporary English Online* and learn their meanings and styles. Use them and change the form where necessary in the following sentences.

| rough | so | show | leave out |
| approximate | hence | demonstrate | exclude |

1. The time ranges associated with these compositions are rather _____, but are in general still perfectly valid.
2. It's just a _____ draft, but I'd like you to read it and tell me what you think.
3. Where rainfall is adequate soil is frequently bad: _____ the rain-soaked, acid fields in parts of Galicia.
4. I was feeling hungry, _____ I made myself a sandwich.
5. The block should be highlighted, as _____ in Figure 10.9.
6. A trainer came in to _____ how the new computer system worked.
7. We didn't mean to _____ the information.
8. The report concluded that far more boys were _____ each year than girls.

❷ The following informal words and expressions are used in daily communication and inappropriate for academic writing. Replace them with formal and academic ones with the same meaning.

Informal	Formal
a hot topic	
besides	
in the end	
really	
(It) seems …	
fix up, mend	
shorten	
understanding	
sight	

continued

Informal	Formal
in charge	
enough	
more and more	
a lot of	
on and off	
at once	
again and again	
worse	
easy	

Project

❶ Translate the "egg sucking" story (Reading ❷) into Chinese. Try to keep the style (wording features) of the two speakers in the Chinese version.

❷ Discussion: What makes a good dictionary? How do you find a good dictionary? How do you use a dictionary?

Lesson 4
Sentence basics

Overview

☑ Sentence structures

- Types of English sentences

☑ Writing: Wrong sentences

- Run-ons
- Sentence fragments

☑ Reading: Long sentences

Sentence structures

Basic concepts

❶ Discuss with your classmates: What are the main sentence structures in English?

_____
_____

❷ Fill in the blanks with the following key terms concerning sentence structures in English.

complex sentence	dependent clause	independent clause
subject	simple sentence	compound sentence
compound-complex sentence		

1. _subject_   A. is the noun, pronoun or noun phrase that precedes and governs the main verb.
2. _____   B. contains a subject and a predicate, and expresses a complete thought.
3. _____   C. starts with a subordinating conjunction or a relative pronoun and contains a subject and a verb, but does not express a complete thought.
4. _____   D. consists of one independent clause.
5. _____   E. is two (or more) independent clauses joined by a conjunction or semi-colon. Each of these clauses could form a sentence alone.
6. _____   F. consists of an independent clause plus a dependent clause.
7. _____   G. consists of at least two independent clauses and one or more dependent clauses.

Types of English sentences

❶ Read the following introduction of the four types of English sentences.

1. A simple sentence
   - consists of one independent clause;
   - contains a subject and a predicate, and expresses a complete thought.
   (1) The traditional Chinese lunar calendar divides the year into 24 solar terms.

(2) Autumn Equinox, the 16th solar term of the year, lies at the midpoint of autumn, dividing autumn into two equal parts.

(3) Spanning across centuries, corn, beans, and squash have been the backbone of indigenous cultures both spiritually and practically.

(4) Offshore wind in particular has huge potential and is forecast to grow by 13% a year to become a $1 trillion business.

2. A compound sentence
   - has two (or more) independent clauses joined by **a coordinating conjunction** or **semi-colon**.

   (1) SPF stands for sun protection factor, **and** it's a measure of protection against UV rays.

   (2) The store must replace the damaged goods, **or** it must issue a full refund.

   (3) Orange blossoms are killed by frost, **but** cherry blossoms still develop.

   (4) Many nouns ending in -or are derived from verbs; they refer to the actor of the verbs.

3. A complex sentence
   - consists of an independent clause **plus** a dependent clause (a subordinate clause);
   - uses **a subordinating conjunction** or **a relative pronoun to** join the clauses.

   (1) **When** the cold air southward meets the declining warm and wet air, precipitation is the result.

   (2) It was estimated **that** about 16 million jobs were created that year.
       (independent clause)   (subordinate clause)

   (3) It would be nice to have a system **that** automatically recognizes numbers and letters.

   [**Notes**]
   - Some common subordinating conjunctions: after, although, as, because, before, how, if, once, since, than, that, though, till, until, when, where, whether, while
   - Five basic relative pronouns: that, which, who, whom, whose

4. A compound-complex sentence
   - consists of **at least** two independent clauses **and** one or more dependent clauses.

   (1) It would be nice to have a system that automatically recognizes numbers
       (independent clause 1)   (subordinate clause)

English Reading and Writing for Academic Purposes

and letters, **but** <u>this</u> is too difficult with existing technology.
(independent clause 2)

(2) **When** <u>you</u> are sent damaged goods, <u>the store</u> must replace the items, **or**
(subordinate clause)　　　　　　　(independent clause 1)
<u>it</u> must issue a full refund.
(independent clause 2)

❷ **Judge the structure type of the following sentences.**

| Type 1 | simple sentence | Type 2 | compound sentence |
| Type 3 | complex sentence | Type 4 | compound-complex sentence |

1. (　) Apple had sold ninety million iPhones, and it reaped more than half of the total profits generated in the global cell phone market.
2. (　) At the end of that time it had lost a third of its weight but appeared quite healthy.
3. (　) Since the Autumn Equinox, most of the areas in China have entered the cool autumn.
4. (　) The report found that spending time on the computer and the Internet was the number one leisure activity for Chinese youths.
5. (　) Closed apps aren't always fully closed, and may continue to work in the background, overloading the processor with tasks and rapidly sucking the battery dry.
6. (　) An assembly line is a flow-line production system, which is typical in high quantity production of standardized commodities and low volume production of customized products.
7. (　) Originally, assembly lines targeted at mass production of single products.
8. (　) With the diversified needs of the customers, the number of product models began to increase.
9. (　) For example, in the automotive and electronic industries, the customers hope to buy individualized products according to their own requirements and affordability, which impels manufacturers to extend the capability of existing assembly lines so as to produce various products concurrently.
10. (　) In such a context, mixed-model assembly lines arise.
11. (　) It specializes in assembling a variety of product models with similar characteristics at the same time.
12. (　) In this work, two selection mechanisms, elite preservation strategy and tournament selection, have been applied together, and it is

executed with two steps.

13. (　　) The number "1" represents that the line is the immediate predecessor of the column, and the number "2" shows that the tasks in the line are sequence-dependent to those in the column.

❸ **Find a journal article in your field, read the abstract of the article, and identify the sentence types in it.**

Writing: Wrong sentences

Two types of sentence errors highly frequent English learners' writing: run-ons and sentence fragments.

Run-ons

A run-on sentence occurs when two or more independent clauses are joined improperly, which is accompanied by misuse of punctuation and missing necessary linking devices (conjunctions or other linking words).

Some 13.2 percent of China's underage Net users are obsessed with the Internet, 13-to-17-year-olds are the most heavily addicted. (No linking word joins the two clauses.)

Improvement:

Some 13.2 percent of China's underage Net users are obsessed with the Internet and 13-to-17-year-olds are the most heavily addicted.

Sentence fragments

A sentence fragment is a broken sentence or an incomplete sentence, which does not express a complete idea.

Some 13.2 percent of China's underage Net users are obsessed with the Internet and 13-to-17-year-olds are the most heavily addicted. 17.1 percent of this age group reportedly obsessed. (A predicate or a verb is missing in the last sentence of this writing.)

Improvement:

Some 13.2 percent of China's underage Net users are obsessed with the Internet. 13-to-17-year-olds are the most heavily addicted, <u>and</u> 17.1 percent of this age group <u>is</u> reportedly obsessed. Or:

Some 13.2 percent of China's underage Net users are obsessed with the Internet and 13-to-17-year-olds are the most heavily addicted, <u>with</u> 17.1 percent of this age group reportedly obsessed.

❶ **The following wrong sentences are from the drafts of some novice technical writers. Based on your understanding of both English sentence structures and types of wrong sentences, tell whether they are run-ons or fragments, and then improve them.**

1. There are several research directions can be studied in the future.

2. In the increasingly fierce market competition, many catering businesses already have owned their own brands, still can not meet the specific and various market demands.

3. According to the survey data provided by sootoo. com, concerning the ordering channels distribution of catering and takeaway in the first half of 2015, mobile clients make up 85%, PC users make up 15%, which shows that the catering users mainly focus on mobile clients, therefore, mobile phone ordering channels should be improved so as to expand the scale of OR users.

4. There were 180 entrants for this contest, the youngest is a boy of 12.

5. Apple is well known for its culture of secrecy, the development of the iPhone was no different.

6. Then I attended Yunchuan Junior High. A junior high that was a rich experience.

7. Some bird feeders are designed to ward off unwanted birds or predators. Such as squirrels, raccoons, bees, and even sparrows.

8. English is used in many situations, nevertheless, this does not mean that people who use it can speak English in all situations.

9. During balancing workloads along assembly lines, there exist certain connections among sequence-dependent tasks, such connections have not yet been studied in the literature.

10. In real practical production, sequence-dependent tasks are common in mixed-model assembly lines. Such as automotive and electronic industries.

_____

11. Concerning the number and amplitude of the original absorption spectra, the nearest coordination number of sample Fe1 (11.47) is smaller than that of the standard sample Fe0 (12.09), the reasons can be the interference of the unexpected Fe-Si bond and Fe-O bond which occur mostly around the surface area of the nanoparticles.

_____

_____

12. At high current densities, the magnesium ions discharge very fast, resulting in the reduction and diffusion of zirconium in the alloy were restrained, and the content of zirconium was low.

_____

13. Libraries are publicly funded, therefore essentially free to the public.

_____

❷ **Fill in the blanks with proper linking words and/or punctuation to make the sentences in the paragraph acceptable in terms of sentence structure types.**

1. How to avoid your smartphones from overheating

To avoid overheating, you need to take care of your phone. It helps to use silicon-based phone cases. __1__ your smartphone is already overheated, you need to remove the case entirely __2__ try to cool it down, preferably with a fan. Don't just put a smartphone in the fridge. That won't help at all! Only use high-quality cables to charge your phone, __3__ don't charge over the max. An extra 15 minutes of work won't make up for the loss if your phone starts to overheat. __4__ it still happens, consider replacing the battery.

2. How to secure a copyright

Copyright is secured automatically __1__ the work is created, __2__ a work is "created" when it is fixed in a copy or phonorecord for the first time. "Copies" are material objects from __3__ a work can be read or visually perceived either directly or with the aid of a machine or device, __4__ books, manuscripts, sheet music, film, videotape, or microfilm. "Phonorecords" are material objects embodying fixations of sounds (excluding, by statutory definition, motion picture soundtracks), such as cassette tapes, CDs, or vinyl disks. __5__, for example, a song (the "work") can be fixed in sheet music ("copies") or in phonograph disks ("phonorecords"), or both. __6__ a work is prepared over a period of time, the part of the work that is fixed on a particular date constitutes the created work as of that date.

Reading: Long sentences

❶ **Read the following passage that explains how to simplify complicated sentences.**

How to Simplify Complicated Sentences

Complicated sentences frequent scientific and technical texts. English learners sometimes find themselves lost in complicated sentences like wrapped in a pile of tangled wires.

Since all English sentences, long or short, are composed of subjects and verbs or clauses connected by linking words, one efficient way to speed reading long or complicated sentences is to reduce them to their main structures. Focus on the essentials or the main structures of the sentences by

- **ignoring the names, facts, figure;**
- **ignoring the modifiers** (such as prepositive and postpositive attributives, adverbs, adverbial phrases, prepositional phrases, etc.);
- **locating the subjects and verbs;**
- **noticing the linking words that connect clauses.**

Take a complicated sentence from Mark Twain's *Life on the Mississippi* for an instance:

When I was a boy, there was but one permanent ambition among my comrades in our village on the bank of the Mississippi River.

The sentence can be shortened in the following steps:

Step 1

When I was a boy, there was but one permanent ambition ~~among my comrades in our village on the bank of the Mississippi River~~. ← prepositional phrases

Step 2

When I was a boy, there was ~~but~~ one ~~permanent~~ ambition.
(but = adverb; permanent = prepositive attributive)

Step 3

<u>When</u> I was a boy, there was one ambition.
(When = linking word; I was a boy = subordinate clause; there was one ambition = main clause)

Now, try a rather long and confusing sentence from a technical text:

It is not that sedentary living causes wrinkles, but that vigorous exercise wards them off by increasing blood flow, which brings nutrients and oxygen to skin cells, encouraging sweating, which eliminates wastes, raising skin temperature, which fosters collagen production, relieving stress, which should reduce frowning and facial tightness, and helping you to avoid the complication of repeated weight gain and loss.

Ignoring prepositive attributives, prepositional phrases & adverbials:

> prepositive attributives
> prepositional phrase
> adverbials

It is not that ~~sedentary~~ living causes wrinkles, but that ~~vigorous~~ exercise wards them off by increasing blood flow, which brings nutrients and oxygen to skin cells, encouraging sweating, which eliminates wastes, raising skin temperature, which fosters collagen production, relieving stress, which should reduce frowning and facial tightness, and helping you to avoid the complication of repeated weight gain and loss.

> linking words
> 2 coordinate clauses
> 4 subordinate clauses (introduced by "which")

*It is not **that** ... living causes wrinkles, **but that** ... exercise wards them off ... **which** brings nutrients and oxygen ... **which** eliminates wastes ... **which** fosters collagen production ... **which** should reduce frowning and facial tightness ...*

Hence, the sentence structures are in this way:

It is not that sedentary living causes wrinkles, but that vigorous exercise wards them off by: ¹increasing blood flow, which brings nutrients and oxygen to skin cells, ²encouraging sweating, which eliminates wastes, ³raising skin temperature, which fosters collagen production, ⁴relieving stress, which should reduce frowning and facial tightness, and ⁵helping you to avoid the complication of repeated weight gain and loss.

So, the main idea is:

It is not that sedentary living causes wrinkles, but that exercise wards wrinkles off.

❷ Cut the following long sentences to their basic structures.

1. Planting bamboo also has advantages for the planet, as the shrub is a grass, not a tree, and is incredibly efficient at absorbing carbon dioxide, as well as emitting 35% more oxygen than trees.

    _____
    _____
    _____

2. Determining the timing of an eruption in a monitored volcano depends on measuring a number of parameters, including, but not limited to, seismic activity at the volcano (especially depth and frequency of volcanic earthquakes), ground deformations, and gas emissions.

_____

_____

3. Even though the name may mean "beside the water", water is extremely scarce, which means a lot of planning and a lot of extra weight for any longer hikes to explore these exceptionally remote and difficult-to-reach areas.

_____

_____

4. Scientists are learning a great deal about how the large plates in the earth's crust move, the stresses between plates, how earthquakes work, and the general probability that given place will have an earthquake, although they still cannot predict earthquakes.

_____

_____

❸ **Group work.**

Are there any long or complicated sentences that have puzzled you in your daily academic reading? Work in small groups and complete the following tasks: i) to share those frustrating sentences; ii) to choose the top three "headache" sentences in your group; iii) to analyze their structures using the simplification method introduced in this lesson.

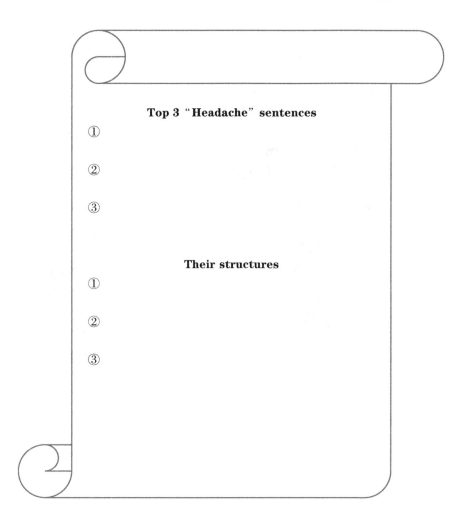

English Reading and Writing for Academic Purposes

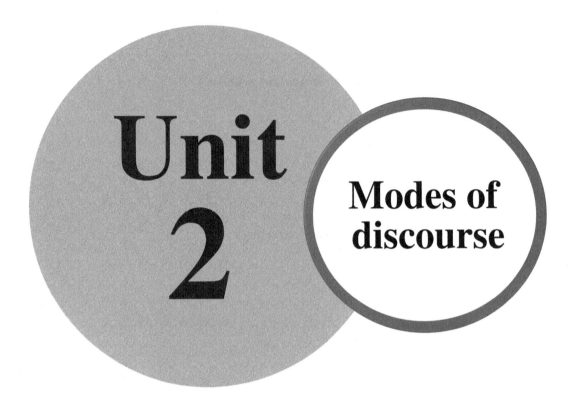

Unit 2
Modes of discourse

Lesson 1
Narration (1)

Overview

☑ Listening

- What is narration?

☑ Reading

- Narration: Point of view
- Is your dog lying to other dogs about its size?
- Narration: Reported speech and reporting words

☑ Academic skills

- Reporting words

☑ Vocabulary

Listening

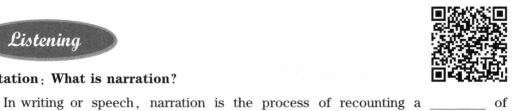

Dictation: What is narration?

In writing or speech, narration is the process of recounting a _____ of events, real or imagined. It's also called storytelling. Aristotles term for narration was prothesis.

The person who _____ the events is called a narrator. Stories can have _____ or unreliable narrators. For example, if a story is being told by someone insane, lying, or deluded, such as in Edgar Allen Poe's "The Tell-Tale Heart", that narrator would be deemed unreliable. The _____ itself is called a narrative. The _____ from which a speaker or writer _____ a narrative is called a point of view. Types of point of view include first person, which uses "I" and follows the thoughts of one person or just one at a time, and third person, which can be _____ to one person or can show the thoughts of all the characters, called the omniscient third person. Narration is the base of the story, the text that's not dialogue or _____ material.

Reading

❶ **Identify the point of view (first, second or third person) used in the following sentences found in scientific texts.**

( ) 1. The study presented here in this report is one of the first investigations to assess the impact of deforestation.

( ) 2. Prior to data collection, the participants received an explanation of the project.

( ) 3. This project was conceived during my time working for X company. As a medical advisor, I witnessed how vaccination changed the situation in the area.

( ) 4. Early in the pandemic, an international team of scientists undertook a comprehensive study to identify human proteins that interact with proteins from SARS-CoV-2. The idea was that if one or more of these human proteins were required for viral production, then there may be drugs.

( ) 5. Be sure the system is properly ventilated for your type of installation. You must vent the exhaust to a safe place, away from people, animals, food handling areas, and all sources of ignition when pumping flammable or hazardous fluids.

( ) 6. If the fluid inlet pressure to the pump is more than 25% of the outlet working pressure, the ball check valves will not close fast enough, resulting in inefficient pump operation.

( ) 7. In this study, we tested the hypothesis that scent marking varies with body size in dogs.

❷ **Work with your classmates to match the points of view with their corresponding usages and functions.**

First person	1. In science and mathematics, this point of view is rarely used compared with other points of view since it is often considered to be somewhat self-serving and arrogant.
	2. If the writing focus is on "what" happened, "how" it was done and "what" was found, academic writers tend to remove themselves from the writing in the interests of objectivity.
Second person	3. This point of view is usually used in the context of providing instructions or advice, such as in "how to" manuals. The reason behind using it is to engage the reader, or push the reader to take action.
	4. This point of view is considered intense, subjective and personal. Thus, it is the natural choice for memoirs, autobiographies, and personal-experience essays.
	5. This point of view is generally used in scientific papers because it reads objective.
Third person	6. In some cases, a researcher may participate in research as a participant-observer. When he or she reports the research, this point of view is naturally used, especially when reporting methods.
	7. Academic texts rarely address the readers directly and the pronoun normally used for this person is avoided.

❸ **The sentences below are from a passage you are going to read. Please read each sentence and write the letter of the word or phrase that is the closest in meaning to the boldfaced word.**

> A. an informal term for a dog—often used humorously
> B. [*formal*] a dog
> C. the yellow liquid waste that comes out of the body from the bladder
> D. unusually or excessively great in amount or degree
> E. a large body/size/weight
> F. capable of moving or bending freely
> G. smell
> H. lift

(   ) 1. The smaller a **pooch** is, the higher it lifts its leg to mark lamp posts, trees, and other objects.

(   ) 2. These exaggerated **urine** streams may fool other dogs into thinking a large **canine** is in the area.

(   ) 3. Some dogs, after **sniffing** a spot and lifting a leg, missed their targets entirely.

(   ) 4. "We spent an **inordinate** amount of time out there," McGuire says.

(   ) 5. Smaller dogs may **hoist** their legs higher in an attempt to lie about their body size.

(   ) 6. By exaggerating their own **bulk**, McGuire says, they could be sending a message to the other dogs.

(   ) 7. Maybe all male dogs lift their legs as high as possible to pee, but small dogs are more **limber**.

❹ **Read the following passage and complete the tasks following it.**

Is Your Dog Lying to Other Dogs about Its Size?
Elizabeth Preston

1 **Don't mess with me**! That's the signal small dogs seem to be sending when they pee on things, according to a new study. Researchers have found that the smaller a pooch is, the higher it lifts its leg to mark lamp posts, trees, and other objects—and these exaggerated urine streams may fool other dogs into thinking a large canine is in the area.

2 "This paper is important because it looks at a neglected aspect of scent marking," Lynda Sharpe, an ecologist at Australian National University in Canberra, wrote in an email. Sharpe, who was not involved with the work, has studied dwarf mongooses that leave scent marks from their anal glands by **doing handstands**; she found that small males leave deceptively high marks. It makes sense that dogs would do the same thing, she says. "It would be surprising if numerous species weren't exploiting the height of scent marks."

3 Conducting the study wasn't easy. Betty McGuire, a behavioral ecologist at Cornell University, and her colleagues studied 45 dogs from two shelters in New York City. The animals, mostly mixed breeds, were all adult males, because they're more likely to lift their legs when they pee. The researchers walked them outdoors in areas that included trees, benches, a fire hydrant, and other tempting targets, while recording from behind with an iPhone. Precisely measuring pee spots before they dried—without disrupting the dogs midstream—was a challenge. And whereas some dogs liked to mark trees and poles, others preferred tall grass, where their urine was much harder to find. Some dogs, after sniffing a spot and lifting a leg, missed their targets entirely.

4 "We spent an inordinate amount of time out there," McGuire says.

5 When a dog made a mark, the researchers measured its height, and then measured the angle of the dog's raised leg from the video. In all, the team analyzed several hundred leg lifts over about 2 years. The dogs' average urination angles, which ranged from about 85° to 147°, got more extreme as the animals got smaller, the team reports in *Journal of Zoology*.

6 Smaller dogs may hoist their legs higher in an attempt to lie about their body size. By exaggerating their own bulk, McGuire says, they could be sending a message to the other dogs: "Stay away from me!" The small dogs may hope to avoid face-to-face interactions with other animals likely to **outmatch** them in a fight.

⁷ **Still**, the dogs may not be lying at all, but instead "overmarking," says James Serpell, an ethologist at the University of Pennsylvania School of Veterinary Medicine. Dogs often like to cover up other dogs' pee with their own, he says. Small dogs may lift their legs higher simply because they're trying to reach a larger dog's urine spots.

⁸ Alternately, Serpell says, the explanation might be as simple as anatomy. Maybe all male dogs lift their legs as high as possible to pee, but small dogs are more limber.

Vocabulary:

pee(撒尿)   ethologist(行为研究者)   mongoose(猫鼬)   anal(直肠的,肛门的)
gland(腺)   fire hydrant(消防栓)   anatomy(解剖,解剖学,结构)
inordinate(过度的,无节制的)

1. **Reading comprehension questions.**

   (1) What does "Don't mess with me" (Para. 1) mean?

   (2) What does "doing handstands" (Para. 2) mean?

   (3) Why does the author mention Linda Sharpe who is not involved with the dog research?

   (4) Why is conducting the dog study difficult?

   (5) "Outmatch" (Para. 6) means _____.

   (6) "Still" (Para. 7) means _____.

   (7) What does the author want to tell readers when she begins the 8th paragraph with "alternately"?

   (8) Based on the information presented by the author, what is the answer to the question in the title?

   (9) Is this passage a scientific news report in a magazine, or an academic paper in a journal?

2. **Understanding narration: Point of view.**

   (1) Is narration used in this passage?

   (2) What story about dogs is narrated? What is the purpose of the story telling?

(3) Is the first person point of view, the second person point of view, or the third person point of view used in the narration? What do you think of this choice?

(4) Can another choice of point of view be possible in telling the same story about the research?

(5) The author does not take part in the dog behavior research, but she presents the results of the research in an objective and convincing way. How does she achieve this? Can you find any evidence in the passage?

(6) Besides right choice of point of view, what else contributes to the objectivity of this passage?

Academic skills

❶ **The art of reporting the words of a speaker.**

Speeches	Reporting speech	Reported speech
Alternative term	Direct speeches	Indirect speeches
Example	"It would be surprising if numerous species weren't exploiting the height of scent marks."	It makes sense that dogs would do the same thing, she says.

Please find all the reporting speeches and indirect speeches in the passage.

❷ **Reporting words.**

Step 1. Read the brief explanation about reporting words in reported speech.

> Reporting speech and reported speech are the two ways we can say what other people have said, written or done. In reporting speech and reported speech, we use **reporting verbs**, or **referring verbs**, to report or refer to other people's words or work. In the sentence "*James said that he was my neighbour*", "*said*" is a reporting verb ("*was*" is a reported verb). In "*Persson (2003) claims that a community is impossible without a shared aim*", "*claims*" is a reporting verb.
>
> The number of reporting verbs is abundant (e.g. the author *says*, *states*, *indicates*, *comments*, *notes*, *observes*, *believes*, *points out*, *emphasizes*, *advocates*, *reports*, *concludes*, *underscores*, *mentions*, *finds*), not to mention phrases such *as according to the author*, *as the author states/indicates*, *in the author's view/opinion/understanding*, or *as noted/stated/mentioned*.

Step 2. Find the reporting verbs or phrases used in the passage "Is Your Dog Lying to Other Dogs about Its Size?": _____.

Vocabulary

❶ **Can you identify any reporting words in the following sentences?**

1. Aaker et al. (2017) argued that non-profit organizations are judged to be warmer than for-profit firms because people perceive non-financial motives.

2. Senauer (2001) proposed that to accurately analyze consumers' food consumption behaviors, it is necessary to account for psychological factors (e.g. attitudes, perceptions) ...

3. Ball (2018) illustrates that buildings that have been persistently vacant may be in poor condition.

4. Chung (2019) reports that landlords are losing interest in going ahead with plans to convert former industrial buildings into hotels, despite increasing visitor numbers.

5. Chung (2006) reported the breakeven period for hotel redevelopment was about 10 years, whereas it was much shorter for office development.

6. In October 17, 2012, Forbes indicated that there were more than 60 million BBM users and 300 million WhatsApp users worldwide.

7. John, Naumann, and Soto (2008) claimed that introverts tend to be withdrawn from others, are less active, and express fewer positive emotions ...

8. According to Wittchen, "social anxiety ... is characterized by persistent, unreasonably strong, frequent overwhelming fears of social performance situations where individuals are fearful of being scrutinized by other people

and being subject to negative evaluation" (2000, p. 7).

9. Reid and Reid (2007) disputed the notion of texting as an intimate form of communication, claiming that lonely young U. K. and U. S. young adults text as a last resort because they do not believe texting increases intimacy.

10. Sean (2013) claimed that the price of home appliances will not rise dramatically.

❷ Use *Longman Dictionary of Contemporary English Online* to learn the meaning, usage and register of the reporting verbs used in ❶.

Reporting verbs	Meaning, usage	Register
argue	[intransitive, transitive] to state, giving clear reasons, that something is true, should be done etc, argue that	
	[transitive] *formal* to suggest something as a plan or course of action→proposal	formal

❸ Compare the ten sentences in ❶ and observe their tenses. How many tenses are used? What are they? Why are such tenses used?

Sentence number	Tense	Usage
1	Simple past: *argued*	a past event/with time phrase
	Present simple: *are*	general rule or validity up till present
2		
3		
4		
5		
6		
7		
8		
9		
10		

Lesson 2
Narration (2)

Overview

☑ Reading

- Experimental procedures

☑ Academic skills

- Referencing & paraphrasing

☑ Vocabulary

- Academic words; Reporting words

☑ Project

- Narration in scientific papers

☑ Supplementary reading

Reading

The following excerpt is from two researchers Betty McGuire and Katherine E. Bemis, who narrate how they carried out their experiment in their academic paper "Scent marking in shelter dogs: effects of body size" (Paper 1). Read the material and answer the questions after it.

Paper 1

We collected data between February 22, 2013 and January 24, 2016, and all walks occurred between 11:00 and 16:00. BM was present on every walk, either walking the dog or collecting the behavioral data; either KEB or an undergraduate student trained by BM assumed the alternate role. We used the shelter's dog walking equipment and followed their walking procedures. Briefly, we attached either a 5 m retractable leash (Flexi North America, LLC, Charlotte, NC, USA) or a cloth lead at least 1.8 m long to a harness (either a PetSafe Easy Walk Harness, Radio Systems Corporation, Knoxville, TN, USA or a Zack and Zoey Nylon Pet Harness, Pet Any Way LLC, model US2395 14 99). We walked each dog to a grassy field (16.6 ha; 42°28_x0005_ 20_x0005__x0005_ N, 76°26_x0005_ 22_x0005_ W) across the street from the shelter.

We allowed dogs to set the pace of walks and scored their behavior during the first 20 mins of the walk. We recorded each urination and whether the urination was preceded by sniffing (a dog stopped walking and investigated with its nose either a location on the ground or an obvious target in the environment, such as a mound of vegetation, tree trunk, signpost, bench, or fence surrounding the outdoor enclosure). We also recorded whether the urination was directed at either the location sniffed or a target (within 20 cm; Ranson and Beach, 1985). Thus, the following three situations would be classified as a directed urination: 1) a dog sniffed a location on the ground and then urinated on that location; 2) a dog sniffed a target and then urinated on that target; and 3) a dog directed urine at a target without first sniffing the target. Some authors consider all urinations as scent marking events in canids (Gese and Ruff, 1997). Others stipulate that the urination must be directed at a target to qualify as scent marking and consider that urinations without a directional quality are simple eliminations (Kleiman, 1966). Given this difference in opinion, we recorded all urinations (consistent with the broad definition of scent marking) and whether each was directed at a target (in line with the narrower definition of scent marking; this definition would exclude urinations on the ground which were not preceded by sniffing the particular location, so called simple eliminations). Finally, we recorded each defecation. Most often we collected behavioral data using a check sheet. On occasion, BM verbally recorded observations using the voice memo app on an iPhone 5 (model ME306LL/A, Apple Inc., Cupertino, CA, USA) and later transferred these data to a check sheet within a few hours of the walk.

(Source: McGuire, B. & Bemis, K. E. 2017. Scent marking in shelter dogs: effects of body size. Appl. Anim. Behav. Sci. 186, 49–55)

1. Summarize how the experiment was carried out.

2. Which point of view is employed by the authors? What kind of effect is created by the use of it?

3. Compare the point of view used by Betty McGuire and Katherine E. Bemis in this excerpt and that used by Elizabeth Preston in her "Is Your Dog Lying to Others about Its Size?". Explain why they have different choices in point of view.

4. In "Some authors consider all urinations as scent marking events in canids (Gese and Ruff, 1997). Others stipulate that the urination must be directed at a target to qualify as scent marking and consider that urinations without a directional quality are simple eliminations (Kleiman, 1966)", who are "some authors" and "others" respectively?

5. Do the co-authors use reporting verbs to refer to other researchers' ideas? If yes, what are they?

6. Are there any differences between the reporting verbs used in the two passages ("Experimental Procedures" and "Is Your Dog Lying to Others about Its Size?")? Find the reporting words and analyze their style in the following chart.

Passage	Reporting words	Style	Comment
Experimental Procedures			
Is Your Dog Lying …?			

Academic skills

Referencing and paraphrasing.

In "Scent marking in shelter dogs: effects of body size" (Paper 1), Betty McGuire and Katherine E. Bemis referred to a second source, an academic paper from Paul D. McGreevy et al. in the following way:

> McGreevy et al. (2013) found that in-home problematic behaviors, which included urination when left alone, defecation when left alone, urine marking, and emotional urination (urination when approached or handled), were more common in dogs as height decreased.
>
> ... McGreevy et al. (2013) also reported that defecation when left home alone was more common in smaller dogs.

If we trace back to what Paul D. McGreevy et al. wrote in their paper, "Dog behavior co-varies with height, bodyweight and skull shape" (Paper 2), we can find the original text reads:

> *Paper 2*
> ... The current study shows that lighter dogs are especially likely to be reported as excitable, energetic and hyperactive. <u>At least some of the behaviors more prevalent in shorter breeds (e. g. urination/defecation when left alone</u>, separation problems, attachment/attention-seeking, and begging) could also be interpreted as infantile or care-soliciting behaviors, although whether these are the products of artificial selection for neotenous behavior (sensu [1]) or early environment [16] remains to be determined. All of these possibilities could, in theory, be tested ....
> (Source: McGreevy, P. D., Georgevsky, D., Carrasco, J., Valenzuela, M., Duffy, D. L. & Serpell, J. A., 2013. Dog behavior co-varies with height, bodyweight and skull shape. PLoS One 8 (12), e80529, http://dx.doi.org/10.1371/journal.pone.0080529.)

We can see Betty McGuire and Katherine E. Bemis take from Paper 2 some ideas that are relevant to their research (the underlined part) and **paraphrase** the original information into "defecation when left home alone was more common in smaller dogs". In this way, they **refer to** other researchers' findings.

Paraphrasing is restating the central idea of a source text while using different wording from the source. Paraphrasing is a basic reporting skill in academic writing, especially when writers want to refer to other researchers' work, or literature.

Common **techniques for paraphrasing** include:
✓ changing vocabulary (word class, word order);
✓ replacing the original words with their synonyms;
✓ using a different sentence structure.

❶ **Compare the original text in Paper 2 with Betty McGuire and katherine E. Bemis's paraphrase in Paper 1, and tell what techniques Betty McGuire and Katherine E. Bemis. use in their paraphrasing.**

Wording in Paper 2	prevalent	shorter _____	when left alone
Wording in Paper 1	_____	smaller dogs	_____
Techniques used	synonyms	_____	_____

❷ Paraphrase what Paul D. McGreevy et al. wrote in their paper in 2013.

1. "Dog owners may be unable to answer some of the C-BARQ questions for a variety of reasons."
   McGreevy et al. (2013) reported _____.

2. "This is the first time we have revealed relationships between height, bodyweight, skull shape and behavior among dog breeds."
   McGreevy et al. (2013) revealed _____.

3. "We employed a unique database that surveyed 8,301 dog owners using the Canine Behavioral Assessment and Research Questionnaire."
   McGreevy et al. (2013) _____.

4. "Alternatively, higher rates of behavioral problems in small dogs may be environmentally induced by the ways in which people tend to keep them (e.g. over-indulged or over-protected)."
   McGreevy et al. (2013) _____.

Vocabulary

Complete the sentences with some of the words listed below.

exaggerate	involve	exploit	conduct
precisely	disrupt	analyse	deceptive
range	average	attempt	

1. Developing countries will remain poor unless they can _____ natural resources to their own advantage.

2. It is easy to _____ the contribution that the reading of books and other materials make to development if one ignores the rich experiences provided by home, school, and peer group.

3. It's difficult to imagine whole group work which doesn't also _____ small group work at some point, but with the advantage that whole group work gives the small groups a focus, a purpose and a context to their work.

4. Putting this more _____, the proper time taken by light to pass to and fro

between two fixed points in spaces oscillates.
5. "Any departure from those plans might well _____ the child's life to such an extent that he would be harmed by it," Mr. Levy said to the government officials.
6. Concurrently two commissions were sent out to _____ a searching investigation into the condition of the southern forests.
7. The sea here is very _____ — it looks calm but is in fact very dangerous.

Project

❶ **Use narration in scientific papers.**

Please work in a small group to read one research paper of your major. Then report the research by using the third person "he", "she" or "they". In your report, pay attention to the four key elements in narration: setting (i.e. the time and place where speakers should actively take their listeners), characters (i.e. individuals who make a situation come to life), plot (i.e. the action sequence of the anecdote), and moral (i.e. the lesson that the speaker wishes to convey). You can refer to the following questions:

1. Who is/are the researcher(s)?

   _____

2. What is the setting/background of the research?

   _____

3. What did the researcher(s) do in the research? How did he/she/they do it?

   _____

4. What did the researcher(s) find out? What is the significance of the findings?

   _____

❷ Find 10 journal articles of your major, read their abstracts and work out: 1) the point of view they use; 2) the frequency of different points of view in these 10 articles. Compare your observations with your classmates'.

Paper	Source	Abstract	Point of view
1			
2			
3			
4			
5			
6			

continued

Paper	Source	Abstract	Point of view
7			
8			
9			
10			
The frequency of point of view		Point of view	Percentage
		The 1st person	
		The 2nd person	
		The 3rd person	
Why is there a high/low frequency of the 1st, 2nd, or 3rd person point of view?			

Supplementary reading

Read the following article and do the exercises after it.

Global Warming Begets More Warming, New Paleoclimate Study Finds

[1] Atlanta, Ga., was rainy in September 2009. Very, very rainy. Water poured from the sky for days. In one 24-hour deluge, more than 53 centimeters (21 inches) of rain fell.

[2] Normally, rain washes off city pavement into gutters. Those gutters lead to storm drains. And storm drains should channel the water through pipes to local rivers and streams. But in 2009, the drains weren't big enough.

[3] Roads became rivers. Homes flooded. Roller coasters at the local Six Flags Amusement Park became submerged. The flood did an estimated half-billion dollars in damage. Tragically, 10 people died.

[4] Most of the rain was due to incoming storm fronts. Rain clouds gathered over hundreds of kilometers, due to winds blowing from hundreds or thousands of kilometers away. Marshall Shepherd initially had bet 2009's excessive flooding was due to these "large-scale weather processes". It was just the weather, right?

[5] Wrong.

[6] Shepherd is an atmospheric scientist at the University of Georgia in Athens. He and his colleague Neil Debbage studied the 2009 flood. They ran a series of models — computer simulations of real events. Atlanta always would have flooded that week, they found. But more rain fell on the city than natural weather patterns could explain — 10 cm (3.9 inches) more. Paved surfaces shoved water downstream. This increased what accumulated on the ground in some places by another 12 cm (4.7 inches). In other spots, they could trace back more than one-fifth of the total flooding to features of the city — the skyscrapers, asphalt and concrete.

⁷ It was an example of the urban rain effect—the role that cities play in where and when rain falls. "Urban regions can not only initiate or modify rainfall in storms," Shepherd explains. "They in some cases may enhance or amplify pre-existing rain systems that are caused by something else."

⁸ Cities, he says, can make it rain.

⁹ As Atlanta and other already warm cities get even hotter, their heat can fuel rainstorms. That excess water can now fall on areas that are increasingly likely to flood. Scientists are working to find out what causes this urban rain. And by staring at storm drains and building basketball courts that flood, they've begun finding creative ways to help all that extra water flow away.

(Source: https://www.sciencenewsforstudents.org/article/warming-cities-may-see-more-rain-and-frequent-flooding)

1. Work out the outline of the article.
2. How many stories can you find in this article? What are they? Retell the stories.
3. Do you believe these stories? Why or why not? What is the purpose of telling the stories?

English Reading and Writing for Academic Purposes

Lesson 3
Description (1)

Overview

☑ Listening

- Description

☑ Reading 1

- Subjective description & objective description
- Description vs. narration

☑ Reading 2

- Mind over machine: An incredible experiment on a monkey
- Description: Verbs, adjectives, preposition

☑ Vocabulary

- Objective description: Introduction, time, change, extent

☑ Drilling

- Describing graphs and tables

Listening

The following paragraph is an introduction to description/descriptive essays. Listen and fill in the blanks.

In description writing, a writer gives his readers a clear _____ of a person, object, place, emotion or event through his observation. The key in description writing is to give the readers _____ drawn from the five senses—_____, _____, _____, _____, and _____. The writer has to put them into words so that he could help the reader _____ his subject. It is like showing the reader around a place so he could _____ the beauty of the surroundings, the freshness of the air, the calmness of the ocean or letting him experience how it is like to be in the soccer field _____ his favorite soccer team during a tournament or dancing with his crush at the prom. More than many other types of essays, descriptive essays strive to create a deeply _____ and _____ experience for the reader by using detailed _____ and _____.

Reading 1

❶ **Read the following samples and discuss with your partner about their main ideas.**

Sample 1

Spring, the sweet spring, is the year's pleasant king;
Then blooms each thing, then maids dance in a ring;
Cold doth not sting, the pretty birds do sing;
Cuckoo, jug-jug, pu-we, to-witta-woo!

—Thomas Nash: *Spring*

Sample 2

My souls, how the wind did scream along! And every second or two there's come a glare that lit up the whitecaps for a half a mile around, and you'd see the islands looking dusty through the rain, and the trees thrashing around in the wind; then comes a h-whack-bum! Bum! bumble-umble-umbum-bum-bum-bum—and the thunder would go rumbling and grumbling away, and quit—and then rip comes another flash and another sockdolager.

—Mark Twain: *The Adventures of Huckleberry Finn*

❷ **Read the following statements and decide which are the features of the above samples.**
1. It is a type of writing that provides a vivid description of a person, place, scene, object, experience, memory, etc.
2. It enables the reader to easily get its physical realization.
3. It is narration.
4. It strives to create a deeply involved and vivid experience for the reader.
5. It achieves the effect not through facts and statistics but by using detailed observations and descriptions.

❸ **What senses are involved in the above descriptive samples?**
1. *Spring*: _____
2. The storm scene: _____

❹ **Read the following samples and answer the following questions:**
1. Are the following samples descriptions?

2. What are the similarities and differences between them and Samples 1 & 2?

3. Which sample(s) is/are objective? Which sample(s) is/are subjective?

Sample 3

　　This is a graph on the borrowing of books at Sutton Wood, Rye Slip, West Eaton and Church Mount. The borrowing of books at Sutton Wood and Rye Slip began at 250 and 300 per month in June respectively. However, books borrowing at Rye Slip fell steadily to around 175 at the end of the period, borrowing at Sutton Wood followed a much more erratic pattern. It plummeted to 100 in August, before then rising steeply to finish at 300, which represented the highest level of borrowing of the four. Borrowing at West Eaton and Church Mount, meanwhile, followed very similar patterns, with both starting quite low at 50 per month, but then gradually increasing to finish at 150.

Sample 4

　　The Shakyamuni* and Prabhutaratna* are seated side by side in the "lotus posture" (*jiafu zuo*) on a rectangular sumeru throne. Both are wearing a conch-style chignon* atop their heads. In creating a symmetrical effect, the two raise opposing hands in the "have no fear" mudra*. They each rest the other hand on the corresponding knee. Both Shakyamuni and Prabhutaratna have round faces, fine facial features, and long earlobes. The sumeru throne is carved with lotus flowers and has

a high base. The base is decorated with twin lotus petal motifs* along its upper edges, which is found beneath a recessed section of the base. Four small posts support the throne at the four corners of the recessed section of the base. The throne is backed with a large pointed halo*. On the back side of the halo is a votive text that records the commissioner's name—Zhang Huiguan, a Buddhist nun—as well as the date of the sculpture's commissioning.

Shakyamuni: The founder of the Buddhist religion
Prabhutaratna: The Buddha of the Remote Past in Buddhism
chignon: Hair that is tied in a smooth knot at the back of a woman's head
a mudra: A sacred and symbolic gesture found in yoga, Buddhism, Hinduism and Jainism
a motif: A single or repeated design or color
a halo: A bright circle that is often shown above or around the heads of holy people in religious art

Reading 2

❶ Read the following passage and complete the tasks after it.

Mind over Machine:
An Incredible Experiment on a Monkey

¹ Something incredible is happening in a lab at Duke University's Center for Neuroengineering—though, at first, it's hard to see just what it is. A robot arm swings from side to side, eerily lifelike, as if it were trying to snatch invisible flies out of the air. It pivots around and straightens as it extends its mechanical hand. The hand clamp shuts and squeezes for a few seconds, and then relaxes its grip and pulls back to shoot out again in a new direction. OK, nothing particularly astonishing here—robot arms are operated by software; the arm at Duke follows commands of a different sort. To see where those commands are coming from, you have to follow a tangled trail of cables out of the lab and down the hall to another smaller room.

² Inside this room sits a motionless macaque monkey.

³ The monkey is strapped in a chair, staring at a computer screen. On the screen a black dot moves from side to side; when it stops, a circle widens around it. You wouldn't know just from watching, but that dot represents the movements of the arm in the other room. The circle indicates the squeezing of its robotic grip; as the force of the grip increases, the circle widens. In other words, the dot and the circle are responding to the robot arm's movements. And the arm? It's being directed by the monkey.

⁴ Did I mention the monkey is motionless?

⁵ Take another look at those cables: They snake into the back of the computer and then out again, terminating in a cap on the monkey's head, where they receive signals from hundreds of electrodes buries in its brain. The monkey is directing the robot with its thoughts.

⁶ ...

1. This passage introduces _____.
2. What scenes/objects/places/people are described?
3. The passage is organized according to _____.
   A. space   B. time   C. importance   D. function
4. The passage gives the movement of the mechanical hand a vivid description. Can you demonstrate how it moves? How does the writer help the reader visualize the movement?

_____

_____

5. Underline the verbs the writer uses to describe the details, e. g. how the robot arms and the dot on the screen move and how the cable looks.

❷ **Vivid verbs, adjectives, adverbs and prepositions are frequently used in descriptive writing. Fill in the blanks with proper words given below (change the form if necessary) to complete the description.**

Verb	pull rise break push strip raise set return appear immerse lose deform impact
Adjective	darker stable out-stretched strange-shaped
Preposition	along around on

1. Tool-use had been observed in chimpanzees in captivity, but many people wanted to know if the behavior existed in wild populations. In order to answer this question, Goodall placed boxes full of bananas in areas where she knew the chimpanzees would find them. Goodall observed chimpanzees in their natural habitat and took detailed notes:
   "After __(1)__ and pushing at the boxes for up to 5 min., each chimpanzee __(2)__ off a stick and __(3)__ it of its leaves. Two individuals then tried to __(4)__ their sticks under the box lids ... None of the three had seen either of the others trying to solve the problem in this way."

2. For this photograph, two initially dry aggregates from different soils were __(5)__ in water. The aggregate on the left is more __(6)__ in water and thus __(7)__ less soil than the aggregate on the right. The __(8)__ color and greater stability of the aggregate on the left suggest that it has higher soil organic matter content than the one on the right.

3. "When a drop first __(9)__ low strength soil, the soil surface is __(10)__ under the drop, __(11)__ a ring-shaped bulge of soil __(12)__ the edge of the drop (Fig. 5-9)."

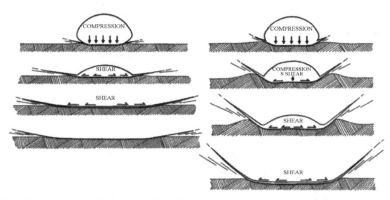

Fig. 5-9 Conceptual diagram of soil splash process for high strength (left) and low strength (right) soil [Adapted from Al-Durrah and Bradford (1982)]

4. The scene is, as usual, a gentleman's secluded dwelling by a river. The house is __(13)__ back in middle ground among trees and bamboo; the owner __(14)__ in the lower right, __(15)__ home from a trip to the market in an ox-driven cart. __(16)__ cliffs __(17)__ above the misty valley.

Vocabulary

❶ The following words, phrases or sentence patterns are frequently used in objective description of scientific reports and academic papers. Please read them aloud and supplement more.

Introductory statement	
The graph shows ...	It is clear from the table ...
It can be seen from the graph ...	As is shown by the graph, ...

Change			
increase	raise	rise	go up
decrease	grow down	drop	fall

Extent of change		
rapid/rapidly	slow/slowly	dramatic/dramatically
drastic/drastically	significant/significantly	slight/slightly

Mathematical expression

half	triple	quarter	average
halve	treble	multiply	total

Time expression

in 1999	in the 20th century	in the first ten years
from 1950 to 1960	by the late 19th century	during the remainder of the year
during the first half of this century		at the end of the last century

❷ **Translate the following sentences into English.**

1. 产量以每年 20% 的速度增长。

2. 消费能力在接下来的十年里保持相同水平。

3. 用户数量增加了五倍。

4. 从条形图可以看出英国从 2000 年到 2010 年信息技术产业和服务产业创造总值在国内生产总值中的占比。

English Reading and Writing for Academic Purposes

Drilling

Describe the following two graphs with the expressions and sentence patterns mentioned above.

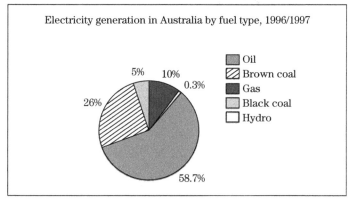

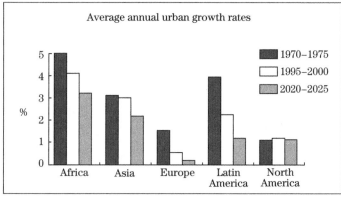

Unit 2 Modes of discourse | 65

English Reading and Writing for Academic Purposes

Lesson 4
Description (2)

Overview

☑ Reading

- Graphs
- Tables

☑ Vocabulary

- Graphs and tables

☑ Writing

☑ Supplementary reading

English Reading and Writing for Academic Purposes

Reading

❶ In terms of graphs and tables, you are supposed to master two skills: understanding graphs and tables, and writing about graphs and tables. Discuss with your partners about which of the following best describes the purpose of writing about graphs and tables.
1. To explain what is in the graph or table in a different way which makes it easier to understand.
2. To give exactly the same information in words, in order to emphasize it.
3. To expand on what is in the graph or table by giving additional explanations about the reasons, etc.
4. To draw attention to the most important aspects of the information shown.

❷ Read the following graph and three descriptions. Then discuss with your partners about which of the three best describes the graph.

Sample 1

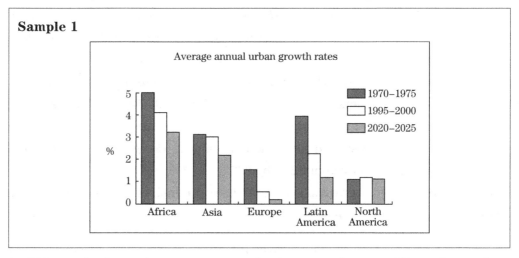

1. This graph shows the average annual urban growth rate of 5 continents from 1970 to 2025. According to the graph, Africa had about 5% average annual urban growth rate in 1970 and over 4% average annual urban growth rate in 1995 and in 2025 the average annual urban growth rate is expected to be just over 3%. For Asia the average annual urban growth rate was just over 3% in 1970 and 1995 and it was expected to be about 2% in 2025. In Europe, by contrast, the average annual urban growth rate was only about 1.5% in 1970 and it went down to about 0.5% in 1995, and in 2025 it will be less than 0.2%. In Latin America the average annual urban growth rate went from just under 4% in 1970 to just over 2% in 1995 and it will probably be just over 1%

Unit 2 Modes of discourse | 67

in 2025. In North America the average annual urban growth rate was about 1% in 1970 and 1995 and is expected to stay the same in 2025.

2. Looking at the graph we can see that urban growth has happened on all 5 continents since 1970 and that it is expected to continue right up to 2025. The most dramatic growth is in Africa, Asia and Latin America, because these continents have experienced the most development and industrialization since 1970, while Europe and North America show less increase probably because they already started being more urbanized. In developing countries many people from the countryside are attracted to the cities to look for work and better opportunities in health and education, but this rapid urbanization is causing many problems and needs to be controlled.

3. The graph shows that since 1970 there has been considerable urban growth in all 5 continents presented and that this trend is expected to continue at least until 2025. However, the rate for each continent has not been the same. The developing countries of Africa, Asia and Latin America experienced the most dramatic growth rates in 1975, with Africa having around 5% per annum, Latin America just over 4% and Asia over 3%. In 1995 these rates decreased to just over 4% in Africa and down to about 2% for Latin America, but Asia remained the same. This growth rate is expected to decrease by about 1% for all three continents by the year 2025. Meanwhile North America is expected to maintain its growth rate of 1% p. a. over the entire period, while in Europe, having started the period at about 1.5%, growth rate is expected to reduce this to only about 2% by 2025.

❸ **The writing about graphs/tables normally consists of two or three parts, which are stated as follows:**

> Generally speaking, the different paragraphs in the whole graph/table essay are directed at **two or three** parts: **Introduction**, which typically gives basic information such as what type of graph it is about and the information it displays, and gives an overview of the trend(s); **body**, which describes the data in detail, verifying the changing pattern, showing the ups and downs, or making comparisons; **conclusion**, which draws a conclusion based on the description of the graphic/tabled information.

> **Tips:**
> When writing about graphs and tables, you are expected to —
> - Highlight the main features of a graph or table, leaving out minor details and irrelevant information.
> - Keep the writing impersonal and avoid sentences like:
>   *I/We can see that ...*
>   *I think it's an interesting feature that ...*
> - Use formal and academic vocabulary, instead of informal or slang words or expressions.
> - Make sure what you say is true according to the given data.
> - Do not give your opinion. You are simply expected to describe the data given.

Discuss with your partner and identify the "introduction", "body" and "conclusion" in each sample below:

Sample 2

The graph shows that since 1970 there has been considerable urban growth in all 5 continents presented and that this trend is expected to continue at least until 2025. However, the rate for each continent has not been the same. The developing countries of Africa, Asia and Latin America experienced the most dramatic growth rates in 1975, with Africa having around 5% per annum, Latin America just over 4% and Asia over 3%. In 1995 these rates decreased to just over 4% in Africa and down to about 2% for Latin America, but Asia remained the same. This growth rate is expected to decrease by about 1% for all three continents by the year 2025. Meanwhile North America is expected to maintain its growth rate of 1% p. a. over the entire period, while Europe, having started the period at about 1.5% growth rate is expected to reduce this to only about 2% by 2025.

Sample 3

The bar chart illustrates the percentages of the gross domestic product generated from the IT and Service Industry in the UK from 1992 to 2000. Overall, it can be seen that both increased, but IT remained at a higher rate throughout this time.

At the beginning of the period, in 1992, the Service Industry accounted for 4 per cent of GDP, whereas IT exceeded this, at just over 6%. Over the next four years, the levels became more similar, with both components standing between 6% and just over 8%. IT was still higher overall, though it dropped slightly from 1994 to 1996.

However, over the following four years, the patterns of the two components were noticeably different. The percentage of GDP from IT increased quite sharply to 12% in 1998 and then nearly 15% in 2000, while the Service Industry stayed nearly the same, increasing to only 8%.

At the end of the period, the percentage of GDP from IT was almost twice that of the Service Industry.

Vocabulary

❶ Judge whether the following expressions are appropriate for the introductory statements and tell the reasons.

The graph/table shows/indicates/illustrates/reveals/represents …

It is clear from the graph/table …

It can be seen from the graph/table …

As the graph/table shows,

As can be seen from the graph/table,

As is shown by the graph/table,

As is illustrated by the graph/table,

From the graph/table it is clear …

> **Note:**
> Writings about graphs and tables in science context are **formal in style**. In order to accord with the style, it is best to **avoid using personal pronouns**. It is better to **use the passive or impersonal constructions**.

❷ Please select the appropriate words or phrases to complete the writings based on the information of the graphs.

slightly less than	finish	reaches its peak
began fairly high	falls drastically	plummeted
fell steadily	no more than	rising steeply
finish	starting quite low	relatively steady
gradually increasing	more	decrease slightly
a greater percentage of		

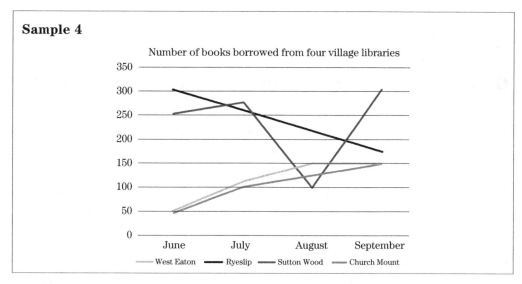

Sample 4

The borrowing of books at Sutton Wood and Ryeslip __(1)__ , at 250 and 300 per month in June respectively. However, while book borrowing at Ryeslip __(2)__ to around 175 at the end of the period, borrowing at Sutton Wood followed a much more erratic pattern. It __(3)__ to 100 in August, before then __(4)__ to __(5)__ at 300, which represented the highest level of borrowing of the four. Borrowing at West Eaton and Church Mount, meanwhile, followed very similar patterns, with both __(6)__ at 50 per month, but then __(7)__ to __(8)__ at 150.

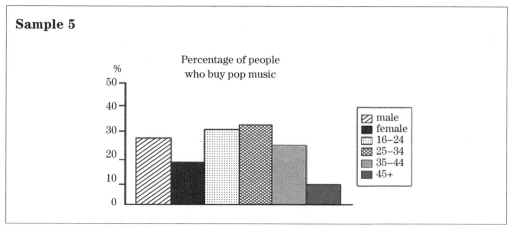

Sample 5

The bar graph shows generally __(1)__ men than women buy pop music and the interest in pop music __(2)__ among the 25 to 34 year olds. Compared to __(3)__ 20% of women buy pop music, __(4)__ men, that is, almost 30% of them buy pop music. People's interest in pop music is __(5)__ from age 16 to age 34, and __(6)__ during the ages of 35 to 44. After age 45, people's interest in pop music __(7)__ with __(8)__ 10% of the population continuing to buy pop CDs.

Writing

❶ Paraphrase the underlined parts with words or phrases learned in this lesson.

The bar chart <u>illustrates</u> the percentages of the gross domestic product generated from the IT and Service Industry in the UK from 1992 to 2000. <u>Overall</u>, it can be seen that both <u>increased</u>, but IT <u>remained at a higher rate</u> throughout this time.

At the beginning of the period, in 1992, the Service Industry accounted for 4 per cent of GDP, whereas IT <u>exceeded</u> this, at just over 6%. Over the following four years, the levels became more similar, with both components standing between 6% and just over 8%. IT was still higher overall, though it <u>dropped slightly</u> from 1994 to 1996.

However, over the following four years, the patterns of the two components were <u>noticeably</u> different. The percentage of GDP from IT <u>increased quite sharply</u> to 12% in 1998 and then nearly 15% in 2000, while the Service Industry stayed nearly the same, increasing to only 8%.

At the end of the period, the percentage of GDP from IT was almost twice that of the Service Industry.

❷ Translate the following sentences into English.

1. 如大家预期的那样，中国曾是最大的稻米生产国，产量约为 193 000 000 吨。紧随其后的是印度，产量超过了 122 000 000 吨。

2. 从饼图可以清楚地看出，到目前为止发电量最大的是石油，占 59%。

3. 1960 年以前，这个数目较小，但 1965 年以后突然增长。

4. 年增长率在 10% 到 20% 之间。

5. 由于灌溉系统升级，该地区的棉花产量比去年增加了两倍。

6. 从柱形图上可以看出，2018 年到 2021 年，学生在购书方面的花费占总支出的百分比上升了 2%，从 16% 上升到 18%。

❸ **Read the following table and describe it.**

	Tobacco related deaths, 1998			Cigarettes consumed per capita, 1995
	Total	Male	Female	
Africa	125,000	112,000	13,000	480
The Americas	582,000	413,000	169,000	1,530
Europe	1,369,000	900,000	469,000	2,080
Southeast Asia	580,000	505,000	75,000	415
India	383,000	332,000	51,000	1,200
Western Pacific	1,185,000	986,000	200,000	1,945
China	913,000	783,000	130,000	1,800

Supplementary reading

❶ **Read the following two excerpts from journal papers and do the exercises after them.**

[1] Located 15 km east of the Lu City at Qufu, a small mound site at Yinjiacheng represents a regional center during the Longshan period (c. 2300–1800 BCE) (Shandong, 1990). Although the mound site has been reduced to less than a hectare by modern destruction, the Longshan settlement at Yinjiacheng produced twenty houses and sixty-five tombs, including some of the largest tombs in the Longshan world. The elite tomb M15, for example, measures 5.8 meters long, 4.36 meters wide, and 1.55 meters deep. The nested coffins were plundered not long after the burial, leaving the skeletons scattered in the

tomb chamber, an example of the widespread ritual violence against elite burials during the Longshan period (Li, 2016). Its grave goods include twenty young pig mandibles, twenty-three elaborate feasting and drinking vessels, and alligator skin plates, likely once attached to wooden drums (Shandong, 1990: 44). The deceased was likely a chiefly figure of a local polity within a short distance from Qufu. The elaborate Longshan ceramic assemblage at Yinjiacheng indicates that this community was part of a close-knit Longshan exchange network or a large coastal confederation (Sun, 2013; Li, 2017).
(Source: Archeology of the Lu City: Place memory and urban foundation in Early China, *Archaeological Research in Asia*, https://doi.org/10.1016/j.ara.2017.02.006)

[2] Zhuangzhi Nanxian Rock Art Site is located 40 km northwest of Jinsong Town. High up on a steep slope, at the foot of a low schistose cliff of 4–5 meters height, occur a few dozen red paint markings. The rock ledge in front of the panel slopes down steeply and tends to be wet and slippery, so the access to the pictograms is precarious. The area over which the rock paintings are distributed is in the order of 7 meters wide. There are few iconic images, notably a relatively detailed zoomorph on the first panel on the left. To the right of this panel occur extensive carbonate accretions, which are 2–3 mm thick in many places and would be well suited for sampling. These run down in several streaks, in a few cases concealing pigment. However, the slippery floor rendered examination difficult.
(Source: Rock art of Heilongjiang Province, China, *Journal of Archaeological Science: Reports*, https://doi.org/10.1016/j.ara.2017.02.006)

1. What do the first two paragraphs describe?

   The first paragraph describes _____.

   The second paragraph describes _____.

2. Explain the following sentences in your own words.

   (1) The elaborate Longshan ceramic assemblage at Yinjiacheng indicates that this community was part of a close-knit Longshan exchange network or a large coastal confederation.

   _____

   (2) However, the slippery floor rendered examination difficult.

   _____

❷ **Read the following passage and answer the questions following it.**

> Shennong was founded in 2006 by a group of engineers who have embraced the mission to design and develop more eco-and-user friendly farm machinery that adds efficiency to Chinese farmers. Focusing on developing harvesters and specialty farming equipment, Shennong builds not only all-electric harvesters but also infinitely clean energy farming products.
>
> In 2008, Shennong unveiled Model Shennong, a small-sized harvester which has better utility for small farms than a traditional huge harvester.
>
> In 2012, Shennong expanded its product line with Model Apple, a capable apple harvester which make apple harvesting easier and more efficient than ever before. In regional testing it was shown to help pick apples 30% faster than with a ladder and with less strain and fatigue on fruit farmers. With one-of-a-kind auto-steering and the capacity to integrate into multiple fruit maintenance solutions, the Apple Harvester is helping local farmers to increase efficiencies like never before.
>
> To create an entire sustainable energy ecosystem, in 2018, Shennong designed and manufactured a unique set of energy solutions, SunnyPack—a facility designed to significantly reduce battery cell costs.
>
> Launched in 2020, Shennong unveiled its cutting-edge battery technology and electric power system: Powerpack and Solar Wall, enabling farmers to manage renewable energy generation. Shennong wanted to prove that electric harvesters can be better and quicker than gasoline harvesters.
>
> From there, Shennong designed her first premium all-electric harvester—Model Fruity—which has become the first harvester in its class. Supporting the latest automotive and energy product are the patented technology twins: Powerpack and Solar Wall. Combining good performance, efficiency and eco-friendliness, Model Fruity has reset the machinery manufactures' expectations for the sustainable energy use in farming in China. And local farmers are operating zero-emission machines in their fields.
>
> With the growth of both the company and the mechanized harvesting market, Shennong will head into the design and manufacture of unique flower machinery, ushering in a green era of mechanized flower harvesting.

1. This passage reads like _____.
   A. an advertisement   B. a business proposal
   C. a company profile   D. a business report
2. How is the information organized in this passage?
3. Is this passage mainly narrative or descriptive? Why?
4. What is the difference between narration and description?
5. Can you find narrative and descriptive part in the materials you read in your field?

English Reading and Writing for Academic Purposes

Lesson 5
Exposition

Overview

☑ Listening
- What is exposition?

☑ Reading
- When it comes to sunscreen, the SPF isn't as crucial as you think

☑ Academic skills
- Expository devices
- Definition

☑ Vocabulary
- Academic words & phrases

☑ Writing
- An expository paragraph

☑ Project
- Exposition in academic papers

☑ Supplementary reading

Listening

❶ Dictation.

Expository writing, or exposition, is a type of discourse used to describe, _____, _____, _____, or clarify. It literally means "to expose". Exposition can be found in writing or _____ discourse. Common examples include newspaper articles, how-to _____, and _____ instructions. Expository writing is also the most _____ type of academic writing!

There are a few characteristics of expository writing you should remember when crafting an expository essay. The first is to keep a tight _____ on the main topic, avoiding lengthy _____, _____, or _____ asides that aren't necessary for understanding your topic.

In the same vein, be sure to pick a topic that is narrow, but not so narrow that you have a hard time writing anything about it (for example, writing about ice cream would be too broad, but writing about ice cream sold at your local grocery store between 5:00 and 5:15 pm last Saturday would be too narrow).

You must also be sure to support your topic, _____ plenty of facts, details, examples, and explanations, and you must do so in an _____ and logical manner.

❷ Listen to "What is expository writing?" and take notes.

Expository writing (exposition)
<u>Examples of expository writing</u>
☐ An encyclopedia entry
☐ A _____ article on a website
☐ A chapter in a _____
<u>Expository writing</u>
☐ Informational, not _____ writing
☐ It is _____ in everyday life, not just _____ settings.
<u>Forms of expository writing</u>
☐ An _____ paper
☐ An _____ for a newspaper
☐ A _____ for a business
☐ Book-length _____
<u>Functions</u>
☐ It explains, _____, and _____.
☐ One of the _____ traditional modes of discourse
☐ Elements included: _____, _____, and _____

☐ The primary purpose: to deliver _____ about an issue, _____, _____, or _____ using _____.

<u>Exposition may take one of several forms:</u>
1. Descriptive/Definition:
   - Topics are defined by _____, traits, and _____
   - E.g. an encyclopedia _____
2. Process/Sequential:
   - This essay outlines a series of _____ needed in order to complete a task or _____ something.
   - E.g. a _____
3. Comparative/Contrast:
   - To demonstrate how two or more _____ are the same and different.
   - E.g. an article explaining the difference between owning and renting a home and the benefits and _____ of each
4. Cause/Effect:
   - It describes how one step leads to a _____.
   - E.g. a personal _____ chronicling a workout regimen and documenting the results over time
5. Problem/Solution:
   - It presents a problem and possible _____, backed by _____, not just _____.
6. Classification:
   - It breaks down a broad topic into _____.

Note: you will want to pick _____ method for _____ piece of expository writing. However, you may find that you can _____ a few methods. It is important to stay _____ on your topic and stick to the _____.

Reading

❶ Read the following words carefully and choose appropriate words from them to fill in the table.

UVB/UVA protection	sunblock	sunburn
fragrance-free	safe for sensitive skin	skin cancer
brown spots	SPF15/30/50	water/sweat-proof
help to stay hydrated		

Problem: Damage to the skin by the sunlight	Solution: Wearing sunscreen/_____	Different choices of sunscreen
_____	_____	_____
_____	_____	_____
_____	_____	_____

❷ **Pre-reading.**

Read the title, the first paragraph and the subtitles of the passage "When It Comes to Sunscreen, the SPF Isn't As Crucial As You Think". Discuss with your partners what the finding about the use of sunscreen is and how the writer may illustrate this finding. Please tick the details that you think may be used in his exposition.

> **When It Comes to Sunscreen, the SPF Isn't As Crucial As You Think**
>
> Buying sunscreen can be a daunting process. Should you get SPF 15 or SPF 70? Spray or lotion? Broad-spectrum, or the fun one that changes colors when it dries? Here's one way to save your skin and save your money: Know that SPF doesn't make a difference as big as you think it does.
>
> **Just a number**
>
> ...
>
> **Quantity over quality**
>
> ...

The details may be:
- Anecdotes ( )
- Comparisons ( )
- Quotations ( )
- Statistics ( )
- Descriptive details ( )
- Definitions ( )
- Charts and graphs ( )

❸ **Read the following passage and complete the tasks after it.**

When It Comes to Sunscreen, the SPF Isn't As Crucial As You Think
By Ashley Hamer, June 18, 2018

[1] Buying sunscreen can be a daunting process. Should you get SPF 15 or SPF 70? Spray or lotion? Broad-spectrum, or the fun one that changes colors when it dries? Here's one way to save your skin and save your money: Know that SPF doesn't make a difference as big as you think it does. What does matter is how you use it.

Just a number

[2] SPF stands for sun protection factor, and it's a measure of protection against UV rays—specifically, UVB radiation. When it comes to sunscreen, you'd think a higher SPF would protect against more UV rays than a lower one. It does, but not by much. SPF 15 sunscreen blocks 93 percent of UVB radiation. Double that number to SPF 30, and you raise your protection to 97 percent. SPF 50 raises it to a negligible 98 percent.

[3] "As you get higher and higher, it's not really a practical difference," American Academy of Dermatology president Dr. David M. Pariser told the *New York Times*. Here's why: Companies calculate SPF by comparing the time it takes a person to burn unprotected with the time it takes for them to burn wearing sunscreen. Therefore, if you burn after 20 minutes with no sunscreen, you should theoretically be able to last for 15 times longer—a whopping five hours—with SPF 15. Sounds great, right?

[4] But sunscreen itself doesn't usually last that long. Sweat, friction, and simple quirks of product formulation can make it wear off, which is why dermatologists recommend reapplying every two hours. That means it doesn't really matter whether you get the SPF 30 or the SPF 100 since the formula will probably wear off before the difference in protection becomes important.

[5] Even worse, products with a sky-high SPF can lull you into a false sense of security. "People who use them tend to stay out in the sun much longer," writes Stephen Q. Wang for the Skin Cancer Foundation. "They may skip reapplying. And they may think they don't need to seek shade, wear a hat or cover up with clothing. They end up getting a lot more UV damage, which, of course, defeats the purpose."

Quantity over quality

[6] What is important is applying sunscreen properly. According to the American Academy of Dermatology, most people apply less than half of the recommended amount. For a full-body application, you should use an ounce of sunscreen, or roughly the volume of a shot glass. You should also plan ahead: Slather it on 15 to 30 minutes before heading outside. Remember that SPF is only a measure of protection against UVB rays. Those are the rays that cause sunburn, but it's UVA rays that cause the most skin aging. To protect against the full swath of sun damage, find a broad-spectrum formula that covers both. Finally, because it's worth repeating: Put on more sunscreen every two hours, or after swimming or sweating. Sunscreen is important, but SPF isn't a cure-all.

⁷ Sunscreen doesn't last forever. If you've had your trusty bottle for a few years, it may be time to buy another to make sure you're protected.

Vocabulary

daunting: *adj.* frightening in a way that makes you feel less confident

spectrum: *n.* a band of coloured lights in order of their wavelengths, as seen in a rainbow and into which light may be separated

dermatology: *n.* the part of medical science that deals with skin diseases and their treatment

whopping: *adj.* (*informal*) very large

quirk: *n.* something strange that happens by chance

slather: *v.* to cover something with a thick layer of a soft substance

swath: *n.* long thin area of something, especially land

Answer the following questions based on the passage.

(1) How can buying sunscreen be a daunting process?

(2) What is "Just a number"? What does this imply?

(3) What may influence the lasting time of sunscreen? How to resolve such disadvantageous influences?

(4) What is people's illusion about SPF of sunscreen?

(5) What does "Quantity over quality" mean?

Academic skills

❶ Signal words in exposition.

Signal words are often used to help writers set down thoughts in different types of writing, including exposition. Some words signal cause and effect, for example *because, therefore, as a result, hence, the reason*, etc.; some words signal comparison and contrast, for example *but, however, on the contrary, while*, etc. In reading, signal words can help readers catch the main idea (and the details).

Read the part "Just a number" carefully and mark the signal words used in each paragraph. Then work in a small group to fill in the table.

English Reading and Writing for Academic Purposes

Paragraph number	Signal words	Main ideas
①		
②		
③		
④		

❷ **Expository devices (methods of exposition).**

There are different methods/devices for writing an expository essay. These include: *compare and contrast*, *cause and effect*, *problem and solution*, *extended definition*, *listing*, *process*, *classification*, etc.

1. Read the first paragraph in the part "Quantity over quality". Figure out its main idea and the method of exposition used in it. Work in a small group to fill in the following table.

	Details	Signal words
Main idea: How to _____ _____	(1) _____ for a full-body application.	_____ / _____
	(2) Plan ahead: _____ _____ _____.	_____
	(3) _____ _____ _____.	_____
Methods of exposition: _____		

2. Read the whole passage again. Find the expository devices used in it.

   _____
   _____

3. Read the following paragraphs and tell what the idea is and what device(s)/method(s) is/are used to develop the idea.

   (1) Atoms and molecules have a measurement called the ionization energy, which simply means the amount of energy required to remove one electron while that substance is in a gaseous state. This term used to be called the ionization potential, but that's no longer used. This IE is always measured starting with an outer shell, moving inward towards the nucleus.

   The idea: _____

The method:____

(2) The human body obtains the energy and nutrients it needs from food. However, our cells cannot absorb these nutritional benefits until the food has been "digested"—meaning, "processed and converted into a useable form". Thus digestion is the complex process of breaking down food molecules into energy and other useful components, which can then be absorbed into the 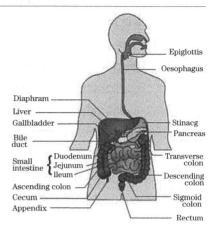 bloodstream and distributed throughout the body to maintain good health. Food remnants which are not absorbed during the digestion process are expelled as waste in the form of feces.

The idea:____

The method:____

4. Read the following paragraphs carefully. Figure out what details are given to explain the topical idea in each. Write down the signal words and key words that help readers catch the details through methods of exposition.

(1) An inclined plane can be made in several different ways. It can simply be a piece of wood placed on the edge of a step, or a log out in the woods leaned against a tree. It could also be a constructed frame 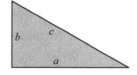 with a horizontal bottom (a), a vertical side (b), and then of course the diagonal ramp or slope (c). The design of an inclined plane will have an effect on how easy or difficult it will be to move things from lower to higher surfaces or vice-versa. For example, moving something will take less work or effort on a ramp with a long distance and a gentle slope. And if there is a steep slope and a shorter distance, it will take more effort.

Key words repeated	Topical idea	Signal words	Methods of exposition

(2) During eating, food passes from the mouth into the esophagus, and then into the stomach from where it enters the small intestine (comprising the

duodenum, jejunum and ileum). Most if not all nutrients are absorbed in the stomach and small intestine. The remaining water and waste products then pass into the large intestine (comprising the cecum, colon and rectum) from where it leaves the body via the anus. Other organs which contribute to healthy digestion include the liver, the pancreas and the gallbladder. A number of important digestive hormones and digestive enzymes help regulate digestion, especially in the upper gastrointestinal tract. The movement of food through the main digestive tubes (esophagus, small intestine and large intestine) is maintained by a series of muscular contractions called peristalsis. Several muscular valves control the passage of food and prevent it from moving backwards. On average, it takes about 40–45 hours for food remnants to pass through the entire digestive tract.

Key words repeated	Topical idea	Signal words	Method(s) of exposition

❸ In scientific and academic texts, definitions are very frequent. A word or a term can be defined in a formal way or a casual way. There are different ways of defining a word:

✓ **A formal and concise definition**:

Word + class/category + characters that distinguish it from others of its class

✓ **A more complete definition**:

Word + class/category + detail + characters(use/features/properties) + examples + (extra information)

1. Read the following definitions, underline the terms defined, and tell how they are defined or introduced.

   (1) SPF stands for sun protection factor, and it's a measure of protection against UV rays—specifically, UVB radiation.

   (2) In climatology, spring is the season of the year between winter and summer during which temperatures gradually rise. It is generally defined in the Northern Hemisphere as extending from the vernal equinox (day and night equal in length), March 20 or 21, to the summer solstice (year's longest day), June 21 or 22, and in the Southern Hemisphere from September 22 or 23 to December 22 or 23 ...

   (3) Preferential flow is the uneven movement of water and solutes through a

relatively small portion of the soil volume at relatively high flow rates allowing these substances to reach greater depth in shorter time than would be possible in a uniform flow situation.

(4) "Public domain" refers to any creative materials that are not protected by copyright, trademark or patent laws. These are owned by the public and can be used by anyone without permission.

2. Fill in the blanks with proper words and necessary information to complete the definitions.

(1) A telescope is a _____ used to _____.

(2) Circus is a group of _____ who _____ _____ performing _____.

(3) COVID-19 stands for _____, a mild to severe respiratory _____. COVID-19 is caused by a coronavirus known as severe acute respiratory syndrome coronavirus 2 (SARS-CoV-2).

(4) Oracle Bones (also known as Dragon's Bones) were the _____ _____ which were used in the Shang Dynasty of China (c. 1600 – 1046 BCE) for _____. The symbols carved on the bones eventually became words and a recognizable Chinese script developed from this practice.

3. The following sentences introduce and compare the geographic terms "weather" and "climate", but they are jumbled in order.

Step 1. Rearrange the jumbled sentences to make a logical outline of the comparison.

(1) Weather is the instantaneous state of the atmosphere around us.

(2) It consists of short-term variations over minutes to days of variables such as temperature, precipitation, humidity, air pressure, cloudiness, radiation, wind, and visibility.

(3) Climate is potentially predictable if the forcing is known because Earth's average temperature is controlled by energy conservation.

(4) Due to the non-linear, chaotic nature of its governing equations, weather predictability is limited to days.

(5) Weather and climate are related but they differ in the time scales of changes and their predictability.

(6) Climate is the statistics of weather over a longer period.

(7) For climate, not only the state of the atmosphere is important but also that of the ocean, ice, land surface, and biosphere.

(8) In short, "Climate is what you expect. Weather is what you get."

(9) It also includes other statistics such as probabilities or frequencies of extreme events.

(10) It can be thought of as the average weather that varies slowly over periods of months, or longer.

A reasonable order: _____

Step 2. Use signal words and appropriate expository devices to develop the above sentences into a logical and coherent expository text that compares "weather" and "climate".

4. Find four to five terms and their definitions in your field. Observe how they are defined.

(1) _____

(2) _____

(3) _____

(4) _____

(5) _____

Vocabulary

❶ Complete the sentences with some of the words listed below.

properly	radiation	volume	roughly
formulas	negligible	recommend	specifically
tend	lull	reapply	formulation

1. For thousands of years herbalists have been using and prescribing herbs both singly as well as in complex _____ usually in the form of tea.
2. In electronic devices, even a _____ instrumental error can totally degrade the system compared to electro-mechanical ones.
3. Eight kilometres is _____ equivalent to five miles.
4. Eggs in the center _____ to hatch as females due to the warmer conditions

within the nest.

5. The wire in the junction box was not _____ covered, resulting in short circuit.

6. Once more, she tries to _____ herself into dreamland via a heroic scenario starring herself and Riva.

7. Their _____ of production was one and a half times greater, and they were engaged chiefly in clothing, woodwork, skins, and agricultural repairs.

8. To apply, submit a curriculum vitae and three letters of reference _____ addressing abilities related to the fellowship.

❷ **Read the passage "When It Comes to Sunscreen, the SPF Isn't As Crucial As You Think" again and use some of the key phrases from the passage to complete the following sentences, where the missing information is given in Chinese in brackets. Change the form if necessary.**

1. This book must be available for all that interested in nutrition and dietary fibre. Food scientists and technologists will find much of interest and value, particularly if they are involved with _____（产品配方）and development.

2. Since language learning is hard work, your early enthusiasm may soon _____（磨掉,消失）unless you are strongly motivated.

3. Their theory argues that political parties, in bidding for support, _____（最终;结果）by promising more than they can deliver.

4. Sometimes we laugh to _____（掩盖）nervousness and to help us relax.

5. Men with a low body mass index in later life _____ relatively _____（保护不受损害）the susceptibility to glucose intolerance（葡萄糖耐受不良）stemming from their low birth weights.

6. Something as small as a brisk fifteen-minute walk each day can _____（很重要,有很大影响）to health.

7. Closure of a scenic spot to tourism for conservation purposes is undesirable, because it _____（事与愿违,违背本意）of conservation which is its preservation for future generations.

8. Chemical sunscreens, the most widely used and available in a variety of formulation, contain one or more of the UV absorbing chemicals that can _____（阻挡UVB辐射）.

Writing

Read the follow materials introducing Bi Sheng and his invention of

movable type printing. Search for more materials about this printing technology at your library or on the Internet. Write an expository paragraph to introduce how movable type printing works with the help of the words provided below.

板印书籍,唐人尚未盛为之。自冯瀛王始印五经,已后典籍,皆为板本。庆历中,有布衣毕昇,又为活板。<u>其法用胶泥刻字,薄如钱唇,每字为一印,火烧令坚。先设一铁板,其上以松脂腊和纸灰之类冒之,欲印则以一铁范置铁板上,乃密布字印。满铁范为一板,持就火炀之,药稍熔,则以一平板按其面,则字平如砥</u>。若止印三二本,未为简易,若印数十百千本,则极为神速。常作二铁板,一板印刷,一板已自布字,此印者才毕,则第二板已具,更互用之,瞬息可就。

(宋)沈括著,胡道静校证,《梦溪笔谈校证》下,上海:上海古籍出版社,1987年,第597页。

Step 1: Read the underlined part carefully and paraphrase it in Chinese.

_____

_____

_____

Step 2: Search out the information in your library or on the Internet. Read the most relevant material and take notes. Present the key information in the following.

Source * 1:	Source 2:	Source 3:
Note:	Note:	Note:

* The source can be part of a book, an article from a science report or a magazine, or a blog article from the Internet. Provide the title of the article, the name of the magazine or the linkage of the website.

Step 3: Write an expository paragraph to introduce Bi Sheng's movable type printing.

(1) Remember to use expository devices;

(2) The following words are for your reference: *clay*, *characters*, *a type*, *a block*, *an iron plate*, *pine resin*, *a frame*, *a wooden case*.

Bi Sheng's Movable Type Printing

_____
_____
_____
_____

Step 4: Check list: The expository devices I used in my text.
✓ _____
✓ _____
✓ _____
✓ _____

Step 5: Proofread your writing and correct the wrong sentences in it.

The wrong sentences in my writing and their improvements:
(1) Wrong sentence 1: _____
    Improvement: _____
(2) Wrong sentence 2: _____
    Improvement: _____
(3) Wrong sentence 3: _____
    Improvement: _____
(4) Wrong sentence 4: _____
    Improvement: _____

Project

❶ **Understand the exposition in academic papers.**

Please work in small groups to read a research paper in your major. Discuss with your group members what expository devices are used and highlight them in the paper. Work out the distribution of the expository devices and then report to the class your findings.

❷ **Surf the Internet for note-taking methods. Introduce common note-taking methods briefly and choose one of the methods and explain how to use it.**

Supplementary reading

Read the article and do the exercises after it.

How Long-term Memory Retrieval Works
By Kendra Cherry

[1] Once information has been encoded and stored in memory, it must be retrieved in order to be used. Memory retrieval is important in virtually every aspect of daily life, from remembering where you parked your car to learning new skills.

[2] There are many factors that can influence how memories are retrieved from long-term memory. Obviously, this process is not always perfect. In order to fully understand this process, it is important to learn more about exactly what retrieval is as well as the many factors that can impact how memories are retrieved.

Memory retrieval basics

[3] So what exactly is retrieval? Simply put, it is a process of accessing stored memories. When you are taking an exam, you need to be able to retrieve learned information from your memory in order to answer the test questions.

[4] There are four basic ways in which information can be pulled from long-term memory. The type of retrieval cues that are available can have an impact on how information is retrieved. A retrieval cue is a clue or prompt that is used to trigger the retrieval of long-term memory.

[5] Recall: This type of memory retrieval involves being able to access the information without being cued. Answering a question on a fill-in-the-blank test is a good example of recall.

[6] Recollection: This type of memory retrieval involves reconstructing memory, often utilizing logical structures, partial memories, narratives or clues. For example, writing an answer on an essay exam often involves remembering bits of information and then restructuring the remaining information based on these partial memories.

[7] Recognition: This type of memory retrieval involves identifying information after experiencing it again. For example, taking a multiple-choice quiz requires that you recognize the correct answer out of a group of available answers.

[8] Relearning: This type of memory retrieval involves relearning information that has been previously learned. This often makes it easier to remember and retrieve information in the future and can improve the strength of memories.

Problems with memory retrieval

[9] Of course, the retrieval process doesn't always work perfectly. Have you ever felt like you knew the answer to a question, but couldn't quite remember the information? This

phenomenon is known as a "tip of the tongue" experience. You might feel certain that this information is stored somewhere in your memory, but you are unable to access and retrieve it.

[10] While a "tip of the tongue" experience may be irritating or even troubling, research has shown that these experiences are extremely common. Typically, they occur at least once each week for most younger individuals and two to four times per week for older adults.

[11] In many cases, people can even remember details such as the first letter that the word starts with.

[12] Retrieval failure is a common explanation for why we forget. The memories are there, we just cannot seem to access them. Why? In many cases, this is because we lack adequate retrieval cues to trigger the memory. In other instances, the pertinent information might never have been truly encoded into memory in the first place.

[13] One common example: try to draw the face of a penny from memory. The task can be surprisingly difficult, even though you probably have a very good idea of what a penny looks like. The reality is that you probably only really remember enough to distinguish pennies from other forms of currency. You can remember the size, color, and shape of the coin, but the information about what the front of the coin looks like is fuzzy at best because you probably never encoded that information into your memory.

[14] Even though memory retrieval is not flawless, there are things that you can do to improve your ability to remember information.

(https://www.verywellmind.com/memory-retrieval-2795007)

1. Work out the outline of the article.
2. What expository devices can you find in this passage? What signal words are used to make the exposition clear and logical?
   (1) expository devices
   - ✓ _____
   - ✓ _____
   - ✓ _____
   - ✓ _____

   (2) signal words
   - ✓ _____
   - ✓ _____
   - ✓ _____
   - ✓ _____

English Reading and Writing for Academic Purposes

Lesson 6
Argument (1)

Overview

☑ Listening
- Argument

☑ Reading
- Facts and opinions
- DNA ancestry tests may look cheap, but your data is the price
- Argument elements map

☑ Vocabulary
- Academic words

☑ Academic skills
- Hedging

☑ Project
- Will you take a DNA test?

Listening

Listen and fill in the blanks.

A strong argument attempts to (1) _____ the reader to accept a point of view. As such, it consists of a proposition, a (2) _____ statement which is capable of being argued, and a (3) _____, a reason or (4) _____ which is supported by evidence. The evidence, in turn, is composed of (5) _____ facts, (6) _____ based on facts and careful (7) _____. If you are analyzing an argument, you should look for both of these: a proposition and the evidence supporting the proposition.

Reading

❶ If you want to write a convincing argument, you need to learn to distinguish between facts and opinions. Put the signal words below into the appropriate columns.

number	corroborate	good/bad	might	statistic
record	verified	substantiate	believe	should
think	eyewitness	point of view	always	prove
guess	photograph	interpretation	never	document

Fact	Opinion
A fact: An actual thing that exists and is provable, observable and measurable.	**An opinion**: A personal belief or judgment that is not founded on proof or certainty.
Facts are certainties	Opinions are disputable

❷ Read the following sentences and decide whether they are facts (F) or opinions (O).

(   ) 1. "The 5G market might be worth over 80 trillion yuan," said Tencent vice president Cheng Wu.

(   ) 2. *Ne Zha* was edited 66 times, with 1,600 professionals and technicians on the job. The 110-minute-long film has about 5,000 initial scenes, of which more than 2,000 were "remade" at the post-production stage.

(　　) 3. "The animation *Ne Zha* was amazingly good. And if something's really good, it doesn't matter where it comes from," Goldman told *Xinhua*.

(　　) 4. Among the 604 Nobel Prize winners for Physics, Chemistry and Medicine, only 19 have been women, accounting for only 3.1 percent of the total.

(　　) 5. Scientific research should be a global undertaking without borders, without gender bias.

(　　) 6. Absolute value of the magnetostriction first decreased with increasing temperature from −630 to 520 microstrain and then increased to a maximum value of −680 microstrain at 400K, and it suddenly decreased with increasing temperature to 140 microstrain at 440K.

(　　) 7. From these viewpoints, this difference of metallic microstructure between surface and inner part results in the different transformation temperature in microstructural viewpoint, and this difference might cause the two-step transformation.

(　　) 8. It is, nevertheless, important to note that we believe the underlying principle discussed are generic in that great inspirations can be drawn to study and improve a large class of catalytic reactions involving light as a critical energy input.

(　　) 9. The analysis of the thermal performance of the continuous furnace for three different radiant-tube designs showed the W-type design was superior to the U-type.

(　　) 10. Nonetheless, we think using hyaluronic acid (透明质酸) is acceptable if one is not comparing between different regions.

❸ **Before reading the following passage, discuss the following questions with your partner.**

1. Have you ever heard about genetic testing? Do you think it is a necessity? And why?
2. What can we do with the genetic test results?
3. How much will you pay for a genetic test?
4. Will you take a genetic test for your family members? And why?

❹ **Read the following passage and do the exercises.**

1. Skim the passage to identify its topic and main ideas.
   Topic: _____
   Main ideas: _____

2. Read the passage again and guess the meaning of the underlined words based on the sentences around them. Paraphrase these words in the blanks in the right column.

DNA Ancestry Tests May Look Cheap. But Your Data Is the Price *Adam Rutherford*	Vocabulary
¹ Do customers realise that genetic **genealogy** companies like 23andMe profit by amassing huge biological datasets? ² In 1884, at the International Health Exhibition in South Kensington, four million **punters** came to view the latest scientific marvels: drainage systems, flushing toilets and electrically illuminated fountains. There, the scientist Francis Galton set up the Anthropometric Laboratory, where common folk would pay 3d (around 80p today) to enter, and anonymously fill out a data card. Galton's technicians recorded 11 **metrics**, including height, hair colour, keenness of sight, punch strength and colour **perception**, and the ability to hear high-pitched noises, tested via whistles made by Messrs Tisley & Co., Brompton Road. Over the course of a week, 9,337 people went home with some trivial information about themselves, and Galton amassed the largest dataset of human characteristics ever compiled up to that time—and a stack of cash. ³ There is nothing new under the sun. In the past decade, millions of punters have parted with their cash and a vial of saliva, and in exchange they received some information about their DNA. Our genomes are a treasure trove of biological data, and an industry has sprung up to sell products based on our newfound ability to quickly and cheaply read and interpret DNA. ⁴ The biggest of these companies is 23andMe: five million paying customers since 2006, usually nosing for clues about their ancestry. Unlike most genetic genealogy companies, 23andMe also offers health-related information, on **traits** such as eye colour, **predisposition** to a handful of diseases, and the tendency to puke when drinking alcohol.	**genealogy**: the study of family history **punter**: (*informal*) a person who buys or uses a particular product or service **metric**: a set of statistics used for measuring something **perception**: the way you notice things, especially with the senses **trait**: _____ **predisposition**: a condition that makes sb/sth likely to behave in a particular way or to suffer from a particular disease

⁵ As with Galton's scheme, 23andMe was never interested in your personal history or your eyes. What it wants is to own and **curate** the biggest biological dataset in the world. So it was no surprise when the company announced a $300m deal with pharmaceutical (制药的) **mammoth** GlaxoSmithKline last month to develop drugs based on the data you paid to give them. This is not illegal any way. 23andMe told users that it was planning to do this, and in 2015 had done something similar, but on a smaller scale, concerning Parkinson's disease. The new deal is the biggest commercial venture of its sort so far.

⁶ This is all unknown territory, and **warrants** serious thought by regulators as well as by customers. 23andMe is unambiguous about its plans: board member Patrick Chung told Fast Company in 2013, "Once you have the data, [the company] does actually become the Google of personalized healthcare. Genomes can be mined for subtleties that only become visible with such **voluminous** data. I've little doubt that interesting science will emerge from this, and new drugs may well be developed to treat awful diseases. I also have no doubt that these drugs will be sold back to you."

⁷ By buying into 23andMe you are not a consumer or user, you are in fact the product. Again, 23andMe was **explicit** about this, and gave all its customers the option of not giving up their genomic data to commercial ventures beyond their control. But of the five million people on its database, more than four million did not opt out, and their data is now fair game. By **tinkering with** some fun ancestry trinkets, you **relinquish** control over information that is unique to you, and allow it to become a commodity to be traded.

⁸ The concerns this raises are similar to many of those created by our new online lives: privacy, **data breaches**, security, anonymisation. It hasn't happened yet, but can genome data held by private companies be stolen, or de-anonymised? Concerns about the potential discriminatory use of personal genomics by insurance companies are well founded. There's no clear pattern of how insurers will or can use information from genetic tests in assessing life cover, but at least in the US, they are entitled to demand medical records, including details of inherited predispositions to particular diseases.

---

curate: to collect, select and present information or items for people to use or enjoy

mammoth: an animal like a large elephant covered with hair, that lived thousands of years ago and is now extinct

warrant: to need or deserve

voluminous: very large, or very long and detailed

explicit: _____

tinker with sth: to make small changes to sth in order to repair or improve it, especially in a way that may not be helpful

relinquish: _____

data breaches: _____

⁹ Can information in these databases be **subpoenaed**? Earlier this year, an open-access genealogy database was used to solve a series of decades-old crimes. The **prolific** American murderer and rapist known as the Golden State Killer was identified after a genetic profile from a 1980 crime scene was uploaded to a website called GED match. Amateur **sleuths** constructed a family tree that within a few days identified 72-year-old former police officer Joseph James DeAngelo, whose identity was confirmed by secret collection of DNA samples from his rubbish and the door handle of his car. The outcome may represent justice long overdue, but the methods represent an ethical minefield.	**subpoena**: (law) to attend court as a witness to give evidence **prolific**: existing in large numbers **sleuth**: a person who investigates crimes
¹⁰ In short: If you really want to spend your cash to discover that you are descended from **Vikings** (spoiler: if you have European ancestry, you are) or you have blue eyes (try a mirror), go ahead. But be aware of what you are really giving up, and consider the potential risks if things go wrong.	**Vikings**: a member of a race of Scandinavian people who attacked and sometimes settled in parts of NW Europe, including Britain, in the 8th to the 11th centuries
¹¹ Twenty-five years ago, the fictional potential of DNA was revealed to the world in *Jurassic Park*. **Resurrected** dinosaurs are never going to happen—DNA is robust, but only over hundreds, thousands, or hundreds of thousands of years at the very most, not the 66m required for a sample of dinosaur genome. In reality, the wonders of modern genetics continue to transform science and society in unpredictable ways. But the moral core of those films—Dr Ian Malcolm, played by Jeff Goldblum—can still teach us something. He is cynical and refuses to be bewitched by the spectacle.	**resurrect**: to bring back into use sth that had disappeared or been forgotten
¹² "Don't you see the danger inherent in what you're doing here," he warns. "Genetic power is the most awesome force the planet's ever seen, but you **wield** it like a kid that's found his dad's gun."	**wield**: to hold sth, ready to use it as a weapon or tool

3. Cut the following long sentences into their basic structures.

   (1) This is all unknown territory, and warrants serious thought by regulators as well as by customers.

   _____

   _____

   (2) Amateur sleuths constructed a family tree that within a few days identified 72-year-old former police officer Joseph James DeAngelo,

whose identity was confirmed by secret collection of DNA samples from his rubbish and the door handle of his car.

4. Read the passage for the 3rd time and answer the following questions.

   (1) What does the sentence "There is nothing new under the sun" (Para. 3, Line 1) mean?

   (2) What does the author mean in the sentence "By buying into 23andMe you are not a consumer or user, you are in fact the product." (Para. 7, Line 1)?

   (3) Why does the author use "again" in the second sentence of Para. 7?

   (4) Find a synonym of "explicit" (Para. 7) in the passage.

   (5) What is the author's opinion about the phenomenon that more than four million people agreed to give up their genomic data to commercial ventures beyond their control?

   (6) What might be the potential risks followed by DNA ancestry test in the author's eyes?

   (7) Who is the Golden State Killer? And how was he caught?

   (8) What does "an ethical minefield" (Para. 9, Line 12) imply?

   (9) What does the author mean by saying "go head" (Para. 10, Line 4)?

   (10) Why does the author mention Jurassic Park?

   (11) What does the author mean by saying "you wield it like a kid that's found his dad's gun." (Para. 12, Line 3-4)?

   (12) What is the point of view used by the author?

(13) How many "I" and "you" are there in Paras. 6–12? Who do they refer to?

5. What is 23andMe? Read the passage again. Underline the facts about 23andMe and paraphrase the sentences in your notebook. Give an oral introduction of 23andMe when you come to the class next time.

6. Read the following argument elements map and work in small groups to analyze the above passage to see if the paragraphs are organized in such a way or not. Label the elements you identify in the margin of the passage, or develop a specific argument map of the passage. Exchange your opinions or compare your map with your group members' and support your opinions with examples.

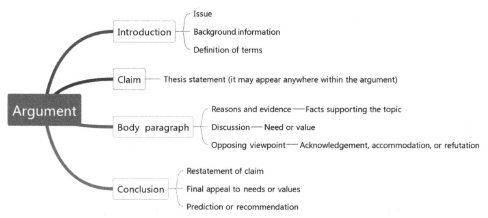

Vocabulary

❶ **Match the words in the box with their meanings given below.**

ancestry	genetic	genealogy	genome
genomics	geneticist	gene	genetic engineering

(1) _____, unit of hereditary information that occupies a fixed position (locus) on a chromosome.

(2) An _____ is the member of your family who lived a long time ago.

(3) _____, all the genes in one type of living thing.

(4) _____, relating to genes or genetics.

(5) _____ is the study of genomes.

(6) _____ is the science or activity of changing the genetic structure of an animal, plant, or other organism in order to make it stronger or more suitable for a particular purpose.

(7) A _____ is a person who studies or specializes in genetics.

(8) _____ is the study of the history of families, especially through studying historical documents to discover the relationships between particular people and their families.

❷ **Complete the sentences with the given words in their appropriate forms.**

theme	thereby	interpret	identify	statistic
thesis	nevertheless	hypothesis	potential	inherent
warrant				

(1) My original _____ that only Washington Nationals employees, Washington Nationals fans and D. C. media members supported the strategy has turned out to be incorrect.

(2) In principle, work and investment decisions become more efficient and _____ raise growth.

(3) The spokeswoman declined to be _____ by name, citing company policy.

(4) "Innovation is _____ in our DNA and will be our calling card in global markets," Mengniu CEO Lu Minfang said in an interview with *China Daily*.

(5) "I derive my _____ from what's happening in everyday life," Ms. Dimoula had said earlier.

(6) In recent years, a growing number of high schools have stopped providing class rankings to colleges, raising questions about the value of the _____.

(7) Investors fixated last year on so-called tail risks, or _____ negative surprises.

(8) _____, Mr. Ostreicher ended up in June 2011 as the only American in Palmasola Prison, an experience he described as "sheer terror".

(9) But people do _____ and observe religion differently and, as Celtics Coach Doc Rivers noted, a fair number of folks "do work on Christmas".

(10) His _____ was neglected for many years because the methodology for detecting such chemical factors in the living embryo was not yet available.

(11) Another area which _____ attention is that of short loan collection in universities.

Academic skills

❶ Compare the two paragraphs below and consider which one is more appropriate for a research article and give the reasons.

Paragraph A	Paragraph B
These results *definitely prove* that plain ethylene-vinyl acetate and cellulose are incompatible. <u>Our results also demonstrate</u> that cellulose fibers are more effective fillers for … <u>No other researchers</u> have previously managed to find evidence of this effectiveness. *Cellulose should therefore be used* in preference to …	These results *would seem to indicate* that plain ethylene-vinyl acetate and cellulose are incompatible. *We believe that our results also highlight* that cellulose fibers may be more effective fillers for … <u>To the best of my knowledge</u>, no other researchers have previously managed to find evidence of this effectiveness. *I would thus recommend using* cellulose in preference to …

My choice and reasons: _____

_____

❷ In argument, especially in technical and academic writing, people use hedging words and expressions to avoid sounding arrogant or 100% certain of the claims. This protects the writer against being proved wrong while recognizing alternative ideas on the subject. Underline the hedging words or phrases in the following sentences.

(1) Interpreting these results is not straightforward primarily because the precise function of XYZ has not yet been clarified.

(2) Although the physiological meaning cannot be confirmed by any direct observation, I believe that …

(3) Despite the fact that there appears to be no clear correlation, I think/imagine that …

(4) One way of explaining these contrasting results could be …

(5) One of the possible interpretations for such discrepancies might be … but our future work should be able to clarify this aspect.

(6) The results did not confirm our hypothesis, nevertheless I think that …

(7) Although many authors have investigated how PhD students write papers, we believe/as far as we know/to the best of our knowledge this is the first attempt to systematically analyze all the written output (papers, reports, grant proposals, CVs, etc.) of such students.

(8) Our results would seem to demonstrate that students from humanistic fields produce more written work than students from the pure sciences and this may be due to the fact that humanists are generally more verbose than pure scientists.

❸ Search more hedging words or phrases from the Internet or documents in your field and take notes.

Hedging words			
Noun	Adverb	Verb	Phrase

Project

Discuss the following questions with your partners. Support your opinions with facts.

(1) Would you like to take a DNA test for yourself? Why or why not?

(2) Would you like to take a DNA test for your future baby before it is born so as to obtain physical and mental perfection? If your spouse disagrees with you, how will you persuade him/her?

Lesson 7
Argument (2)

Overview

☑ Listening

- Discussion in academic writing

☑ Reading

- Reading of the discussion section in journal papers
- Moves in discussion

☑ Vocabulary

- Academic words in discussion

Listening

Listen and fill in the blanks.

The term "discussion" has a variety of meanings in English. In academic writing, however, it usually refers to two types of activity:
- considering both sides of an issue, or question before reaching a conclusion;
- considering the (1)_____ of research and the (2)_____ of these.

Discussion sections in dissertations and research articles are probably the most complex sections in terms of their (3)_____. They normally (4)_____ around a "statement of result" or an important (5)"_____". As there is usually more than one result, discussion sections are often structured into a series of discussion cycles.

Reading

❶ Before reading, exchange your impressions of "the discussion section in academic writing" with your partners and then share your ideas with the class.

	Impression of discussion	Similarity
I		
Student A		
Student B		
Student C		

❷ Read the following discussion section from a research article in the field of applied psychology. And then do the exercises.

	Age, Experience, and Performance on Speed and Skill Jobs
Original hypothesis	[1] The decremental theory of aging led us to infer that older workers in speed jobs would have poorer performance, greater absenteeism, and more accidents compared with other workers.
Findings	[2] The findings, however, go against the theory. [3] The older workers generally earned more, were absent less, had fewer accidents, and had less turnover than younger workers.
Explanation for findings	[4] One possible conclusion is that the requirements of the speed jobs in the light manufacturing industry under study do not make physical demands on the older workers to the limits of their reserve capacity. [5] The competence and experience of the older workers in these specific jobs may have compensated for their reduced stamina.

Limitation	⁶This study has taken a step in the direction of defining the relationship between age, experience, and productivity in one particular industry. ⁷It is possible of course that other industries with a different complex of speed jobs and skill jobs may produce entirely different results. ⁸In addition, it is important to emphasize that methodological problems in the research design limit our interpretations.
Need for further research	⁹The approach outlined in this study should be replicated in other manufacturing plants, as well as in other occupational areas in light, medium, and heavy industries in order to construct a typology of older worker performance in a variety of jobs.

1. Match the words below with their definitions.

    (1) hypothesis   A. a situation in which people are not at school or work when they should be

    (2) decremental   B. the physical or mental strength to do something for a long time, esp. something difficult

    (3) absenteeism   C. to copy or repeat something

    (4) turnover   D. an idea or explanation for something that is based on known facts but has not yet been proven

    (5) compensate   E. to provide something to reduce the effect of something that has been lost or damaged

    (6) stamina   F. a gradual decrease in quality or quantity

    (7) methodological   G. the rate at which employees leave a company and are replaced

    (8) interpretation   H. the study of types, or a system of dividing things into types

    (9) replicate   I. an explanation or opinion of what something means

    (10) typology   J. relating to the method used for doing, teaching, or studying something

2. Discuss the following questions with your partner.

    (1) What was compared in the study?

    (2) What did the authors of this study find out about their original hypothesis?

    (3) Why do you think the authors ordered the information in their discussion in the way shown here?

    (4) What other kinds of information do you think the authors could have included in this section?

❸ In some contexts, the discussion sections in academic writing are entitled "conclusions". Whatever the titles are, the writing conventions reflect some common moves, or steps of writing. Read the common moves in the discussion sections in academic articles and do the exercises.

Moves in the discussion sections		
Move 1	Background information (research purpose, theory, methodology)	Optional, but PISF *
Move 2	Summarizing and reporting key results	Obligatory
Move 3	Commenting on the key results (making claims, explaining the results, comparing the new work with the previous studies, offering alternative explanations)	Obligatory
Move 4	Stating the limitations of the study	Optional, but PISF
Move 5	Making recommendations for future implementation and/or for future research	Optional

* PISF = probable in some fields

1. Read the following discussion section of a research article and identify the moves for every sentence.

> **Discussion and Conclusion**
>
> ¹ Prediction of continental ancestry from genetic sequences have been studied for years. ² However, much less has been done on prediction of ancestry for closely-related sub-populations, for instance, those that are within the same country, or continent, especially under resource constraints, with potentially limited or missing genomic data. ³ In this work, we have developed an ancestry identification system to predict the continental origin of an unknown individual and also distinguish between closely-related sub-populations within a continent. ⁴ We used only SNPs from just one chromosome (namely, Chromosome 1) for our analysis, and to identify different panels of ancestry informative SNPs. ⁵ We have applied both machine learning and statistical techniques to select candidate SNPs. ⁶ Our results show that one single chromosome (Chromosome 1, in this case), if carefully analyzed, could hold enough information for accurate estimation of human biogeographical ancestry. ⁷ This has a significant implication in terms of the computational resources required for analysis of ancestry, and in the applications of such analyses, such as in studies of genetic diseases, forensics, and biometrics.
>
> ⁸ We have essentially considered binary classification, given pairs of sub-populations. ⁹ Further work can be performed to extend the proposed approach to handle multi-class

classification of biogeographical ancestry. [10] Another interesting future work is to investigate the performance of other chromosomes, especially the smaller chromosomes, to see if we can construct equally high-performing panels of AISNPs using an even less amount of data. [11] It will also be interesting to further investigate the identified SNPs to see if there is any connection between them, or their nearby genes, with specific diseases or health problems that are known to be more prevalent in certain geographic regions.

Move 1: _____
Move 2: _____
Move 3: _____
Move 4: _____
Move 5: _____

2. Read the two paragraphs about malaria prevention measures, and then decide which one is better for the beginning part of the discussion.

Paragraph A:

We trapped and counted the number of mosquitoes within the urban environment of the city of Caracas using conventional carbon dioxide traps. Nearly 70% higher numbers of adult Aedes aegypti were caught in settlements in the vicinity of irrigated urban agricultural sites compared to control areas without irrigated urban agriculture. When we evaluated malaria episode reports from people living in various parts of the city, we found that 18% of malaria cases were reported by people living in the vicinity of urban agricultural areas in the rainy as well as dry seasons, whereas only 2% of the control groups reported incidences of malaria per year.

Paragraph B:

The results of this study show that open-space irrigated vegetable fields in Caracas can provide suitable breeding sites for Aedes aegypti. This is reflected in higher numbers of adult Aedes aegypti in settlements in the vicinity of irrigated urban agricultural sites compared to control areas without irrigated urban agriculture. In addition, people living in the vicinity of urban agricultural areas reported more malaria episodes than the control group in the rainy as well as dry seasons. Apparently, the informal irrigation sites of the urban agricultural locations create rural spots within the city of Caracas in terms of potential mosquito breeding sites.

3. Read the two paragraphs about desert frogs, and then decide which one is better for the concluding part of the discussion.

Paragraph A:
   In conclusion, this study shows that desert frogs can avoid death by desiccation by maintaining a high body water content and water storage in their urinary bladder and by rapid hydration when water is available. These measures may be employed in combination with behavioral adaptations such as burrowing and change in pigmentation to minimize stresses tending to dehydrate the animals.

Paragraph B:
   A limitation of this study was the small number of animals, a single species of frogs, and the location of the study area, which took place in only one oasis in the Mohave Desert. Future studies should be extended to other species, a large number of animals, and to a greater diversity of locations.

❹ Read "Things to avoid in the discussion" and the sentence pairs after it. Compare the pairs, identify the problems with Sentence As, and point out why Sentence Bs are more effective by referring to "Things to avoid in the discussion".

Things to avoid in the discussion
1. Lack clarity
2. Overpresentation of the results
3. Overstatement
4. Unwarranted speculation
5. Inflation of the importance of the findings
6. Tangential issues
7. Conclusions that are not supported by the data
8. Inclusion of the "take-home"; save this for the conclusions section

1. A. Therefore, accuracy of Ebb's data is obviously doubtable and should be reevaluated.
   B. Our results do not agree with those of previous studies (Ebb, 2007).
2. A. The influence of counter ions is obvious in Figure 3B.
   B. Counter ions influenced X by ...(Figure 3B).
3. A. Our future studies may reveal how certain single-point mutations affect the conformation of the protein and thus its interaction with the receptor.
   B. Certain single-point mutations may affect the conformation of the protein and thus its interaction with the receptor.

4. A. The model proposed here however is currently an experimentally under-determined system.

   B. Certain single point mutations may affect the conformation of the protein and thus its interaction with the receptor.

5. A. Crohn's disease incidence showed two peak periods: Rates are the highest in young people and the elderly.

   B. In our study we observed a bimodal distribution of Crohn's disease incidence with two peaks in the age groups of 20 to 29 years and older than 60 years.

Vocabulary

Complete the sentences with the words in their appropriate form.

coherently	consistent	understandable	principal
successively	include	substantial	correspond
comprehensible	regardless	independently	process

1. Our results are _____ with previous findings that also indicated that X is greater than Y.
2. The stock market has made _____ gains since the end of the economic crisis.
3. In its current form, the abstract is not _____. It needs rewriting so that readers can immediately understand the contribution of the authors' work.
4. A preliminary study was made of the correlation between acupuncture points for the treatment of back pain and the _____ points revealed by X-rays.
5. A total of 70% of the curriculums were found to obtain from medium to strong exaggerations in terms of skills and competencies. Such behavior among candidates is _____, however, it is not to be encouraged.
6. The two research studies were carried out _____, thus without any collaboration. However, both reached the same results.
7. Table 1 shows the outcomes for all patients in that age category, _____ of the treatment received.
8. These equations are solved _____ by an iterative algorithm.
9. Details are _____ in the supplementary materials.
10. The data were _____ using StAT 2.0.

Lesson 8
Journal paper reading

Overview

☑ Reading

- Scent marking in shelter dogs: effects of body size

☑ Comparison

- A news report & a journal paper
- Register & style

Reading

① Reading comprehension: Read the following academic paper "Scent marking in shelter dogs: effects of body size" and work out the outline of the paper.

Applied Animal Behaviour Science 186 (2017) 49–55

Contents lists available at ScienceDirect

Applied Animal Behaviour Science

journal homepage: www.elsevier.com/locate/applanim

Scent marking in shelter dogs: effects of body size

Betty McGuire[a,*], Katherine E. Bemis[b]

[a] Department of Ecology and Evolutionary Biology, Cornell University, Ithaca, NY 14853, USA
[b] Department of Natural Resources, Cornell University, Ithaca, NY 14853, USA

ARTICLE INFO

Article history:
Received 20 March 2016
Received in revised form 16 October 2016
Accepted 2 November 2016
Available online 11 November 2016

Keywords:
Dog
Scent marking
Urination
Defecation
Body size
Shelter

ABSTRACT

Placing scent marks in the environment allows individuals to transfer information without direct interactions. Given that body size often indicates competitive ability, small individuals may preferentially communicate via scent marking because direct social interactions are potentially costly. However, most evidence indicates a positive relationship between competitive ability and frequency of scent marking. Domestic dogs (*Canis lupus familiaris*) exhibit extreme morphological variation, which allowed us to examine whether scent-marking behavior varied with body size in shelter dogs. We observed 281 dogs on 20-min walks and recorded total urinations, urinations directed at targets in the environment, and defecations. Some dogs were walked once and others multiple times (total walks, 619). We found that size class influenced rate of urination ($P = 0.002$): small dogs urinated at higher rates (0.36 urinations per min) than both medium (0.26) and large dogs (0.24). There was a tendency for size class to influence percent of directed urinations ($P = 0.057$): small dogs directed more of their urinations at targets in the environment (72%) than did large dogs (60%). Consistent with previous reports, we found that males urinated at higher rates (0.41) than females (0.18; $P < 0.0001$), and directed more of their urinations (males, 87%; females, 45%; $P < 0.0001$). Body size and sex did not influence likelihood of defecation during a walk. Defecation is thought to play a less important role than urination in scent marking in dogs, so the absence of size and sex differences in likelihood of defecation was not surprising. Time spent at the shelter positively influenced rate of urination ($P = 0.0005$), percent of directed urinations ($P = 0.005$), and likelihood of defecation ($P = 0.006$), which we interpret as resulting from the dogs becoming increasingly familiar and more comfortable with us. Our findings regarding body size and urinary behavior support the hypothesis that small dogs communicate more frequently via scent marking than larger dogs. Body size is known to influence visual and auditory communication in mammals, and our data show that body size also influences chemical communication. Finally, our results provide context for problematic marking behaviors in the home.

© 2016 Elsevier B.V. All rights reserved.

1. Introduction

Scent marking, a common form of communication in mammals, is remarkably indirect: one individual places a mark in the environment that another individual might encounter, typically in the absence of the individual that placed the mark (Gosling and Roberts, 2001). Information gleaned from the chemical composition of scent marks may include individual identity, age, sex, reproductive state, and social status; and height of the mark may provide information on body size (Sharpe, 2015, and references therein). One advantage of this indirect transfer of information is that individuals can evaluate one another while often avoiding potentially dangerous direct interactions (Sharpe, 2015). Given that body size usually reflects competitive ability (Huntingford and Turner, 1987), communicating via scent marks might be particularly important to small individuals, for whom direct encounters could be especially costly (e.g., fighting can cause serious injury and body size often influences the outcome of fights, with smaller individuals losing; Archer, 1988). Most evidence, however, indicates a positive relationship between competitive ability and scent marking (Gosling and Roberts, 2001; Hurst and Beynon, 2004; Johnson, 1973).

Few studies have investigated whether scent marking behavior of mammals varies in relation to body size. In dwarf mongooses (*Helogale parvula*), which use a handstand posture to deposit anogenital secretions on vertical targets in their home range, height of scent mark and body size were positively correlated for females (Sharpe et al., 2012). In contrast, smaller males marked higher on targets than did larger males of similar age, perhaps indicating an

* Corresponding author.
  E-mail address: bam65@cornell.edu (B. McGuire).

http://dx.doi.org/10.1016/j.applanim.2016.11.001
0168-1591/© 2016 Elsevier B.V. All rights reserved.

effort by small males to exaggerate their size to rivals outside their group (Sharpe et al., 2012). Mice (*Mus musculus*) mark with urine and secretions from anal glands. When two male mice were housed together under laboratory conditions and briefly separated by a divider, dominant males that were smaller than their cagemate, marked more frequently and had larger preputial glands (the source of some components of the scent marks) than did dominant males that were larger than their cagemate (females were not studied; Gosling et al., 2000). These data suggest that male mice adjust their investment in scent marking based on their body size relative to that of a rival.

Scent marking has been studied in detail in several members of Canidae. Possible functions range from defending a territory (free-ranging dogs: Cafazzo et al., 2012; Pal, 2003; coyotes: Gese and Ruff, 1997; gray wolves: Peters and Mech, 1975) to providing olfactory and possibly visual landmarks, which aid in orientation and making objects within territories more familiar (free-ranging dogs: Cafazzo et al., 2012; Pal, 2003; coyotes: Gese and Ruff, 1997) to indicating characteristics of food, such as location, ownership, or that a cache is empty (free-ranging dogs: Cafazzo et al., 2012; Pal, 2003; coyotes: Harrington, 1982; gray wolves: Harrington, 1981; red foxes: Henry, 1977). With respect to social interactions, scent marking may establish or reinforce social status (companion dogs: Lisberg and Snowdon, 2011; free-ranging dogs: Cafazzo et al., 2012; coyotes: Gese and Ruff, 1997; gray wolves: Peterson et al., 2002; bush dogs (*Speothos venaticus*): Biben, 1982) and bonds between members of a breeding pair (coyotes: Gese and Ruff, 1997; gray wolves: Rothman and Mech, 1979; bush dogs: Porton, 1983). Finally, scent marks may indicate female reproductive state (companion dogs: Wirant et al., 2007; free-ranging dogs: Cafazzo et al., 2012; Pal, 2003). Comparative rates of urination and defecation by individuals of different sex, age, social status, or reproductive state typically serve as evidence for particular functions; some evidence focuses on rates of urination and defecation (or distribution of these scent marks) in different environmental contexts, such as at the boundaries versus the interior of a territory and at sites used for courtship versus raising young.

Domestic dogs (*Canis lupus familiaris*) exhibit extreme morphological variation and offer an opportunity to examine whether scent-marking behavior varies with body size. Marking with urine is sexually dimorphic in mature dogs: when compared with females, males urinate and countermark (mark on or near existing scent marks) more frequently, and direct more of their urinations at targets in the environment, typically using the raised-leg posture (females usually squat; Beach, 1974; Bekoff, 1979; Lisberg and Snowdon, 2011; Martins and Valle, 1948; McGuire, 2016; Sprague and Anisko, 1973; Wirant and McGuire, 2004). Sex differences do not characterize defecation, which is thought to play much less of a role than urination in canine scent marking (Cafazzo et al., 2012; McGuire, 2016; Sprague and Anisko, 1973). To our knowledge, only one study has examined relationships between urination, defecation, and body size in dogs. McGreevy et al. (2013) investigated correlations between 33 behavioral traits and height and body mass in 49 dog breeds. The behavioral traits included, for example, several categories pertaining to fear, aggression, separation from owner, and excitability, as well as problematic behaviors concerning urination and defecation. Behavioral scores were obtained from the Canine Behavioral Assessment and Research Questionnaire (C-BARQ), which is completed online by dog owners. McGreevy et al. (2013) found that in-home problematic behaviors, which included urination when left alone, defecation when left alone, urine marking, and emotional urination (urination when approached or handled), were more common in dogs as height decreased. Of these four behavioral characteristics, only emotional urination correlated with body mass, and this relationship was positive. We have found no information on how body size influences behavior associated with urination or defecation when dogs are outside the home.

In this study, we tested the hypothesis that scent marking varies with body size in dogs. We also examined how scent marking varies with sex and time spent at the shelter. We recorded scent-marking behavior of 281 shelter dogs during walks in a nearby field; some dogs were walked once and others multiple times. Given that direct social interactions may be particularly costly to small individuals (Sharpe, 2015), we predicted that small dogs would be more likely to communicate via scent marking than larger dogs. Specifically, we predicted that small dogs would urinate at higher rates and direct more of their urinations at targets in the environment than would larger dogs. Based on existing information (Beach, 1974; Bekoff, 1979; McGuire 2016; Ranson and Beach, 1985), we predicted that male dogs would urinate at higher rates and direct more of their urinations at targets in the environment than would female dogs. Defecation seems to plays little role in scent marking for most dogs (Cafazzo et al., 2012; McGuire, 2016; Sprague and Anisko, 1973), so we predicted that likelihood of defecation would not vary in relation to body size or sex. Time spent at this shelter did not significantly influence scent-marking behavior during first walks of dogs (McGuire, 2016); thus, we predicted that rate of urination, percent of directed urinations, and likelihood of defecation would not vary in relation to time spent at this shelter, now that some dogs had multiple walks.

2. Material and methods

2.1. Dogs and housing

We observed 281 mostly mixed breed dogs (n = 158 males; n = 123 females) during walks at the Tompkins County SPCA in Ithaca, NY, USA. Dogs had been surrendered by owners, picked up as strays, or transferred from other shelters. The data included here represent a subset of those presented in a previous analysis of how sex and age class (juvenile, adult, and senior) influenced scent-marking behavior during first walks of 500 dogs at two animal shelters (McGuire, 2016), plus an additional 15 dogs observed after the first study ended. Included in the subset from the first study are mature dogs (adults and seniors) from only one of the two shelters (the other shelter, the Cortland Community SPCA in Cortland NY, had too few small dogs for inclusion); we excluded juveniles because they are still growing, and differ dramatically from mature dogs in their marking behavior (McGuire, 2016; Ranson and Beach, 1985). All dogs included here were at least 1 year of age (Mean ± SD, 4.2 ± 3.0 years; range, 1–14 years). Finally, whereas the first study included data collected during first walks of dogs, the present study includes data from first walks as well as from any subsequent walks of individual dogs.

Řezáč et al. (2011) used a system of size classes for dogs based on breed standards set forth by the Fédération Cynologique Internationale (FCI), an international federation of kennel clubs: small dog, <30 cm at withers; medium dog, 30–50 cm at withers; large dog, >50 cm at withers. Applying breed standards to the diverse population of shelter dogs is challenging because most are mixed breeds and the few apparent pure bred dogs may not meet breed standards. We used a modification of the system used by Řezáč et al. (2011) because several dogs (10 males and 6 females) were between 30 and 33 cm at withers and resembled breeds typically considered small (e.g., Chihuahua, Pug, Shih Tzu, and Pomeranian). These 16 dogs ranged in body mass from 4.3 to 9.1 kg, which was well within that of the 49 dogs <30 cm at withers (2.0–13.2 kg). Thus, we assigned size classes as follows: small dogs, ≤33 cm at withers (39 males and 26 females); medium dogs, 34–50 cm at withers (39 males and 52 females); and large dogs, >50 cm at withers (80 males and 45 females). For all 281 dogs, mean height at withers (±SD) was 46.0 ± 13.8 cm (range, 19.1–76.2 cm), and mean body mass (±SD) was 20.6 ± 11.5 kg (range, 2.0–53.1 kg).

Details of care and housing have been described elsewhere (Gough and McGuire, 2015; McGuire, 2016); we provide a brief description here. All dogs had been examined by a veterinarian, behaviorally evaluated by shelter staff (Bollen and Horowitz, 2008; Sternberg, 2006), and were on the adoption floor by the time we walked them. Dogs were typically housed individually in one of 13 cubicles (from 5.2 m^2 to 7.3 m^2), each of which contained a water bowl, raised bed, blanket, and toys. Shelter staff fed the dogs each day between 08:00 and 09:00 h and again between 15:00 and 16:00 h. Several times a day, dogs were either taken to a large outdoor enclosure or walked by volunteers or staff. We randomly selected dogs that had not been out of their cubicle (either for a walk or time in the outdoor enclosure) for at least 2 h.

2.2. Experimental procedures

We collected data between February 22, 2013 and January 24, 2016, and all walks occurred between 11:00 and 16:00 h. BM was present on every walk, either walking the dog or collecting the behavioral data; either KEB or an undergraduate student trained by BM assumed the alternate role. We used the shelter's dog walking equipment and followed their walking procedures. Briefly, we attached either a 5 m retractable leash (Flexi North America, LLC, Charlotte, NC, USA) or a cloth lead at least 1.8 m long to a harness (either a PetSafe Easy Walk Harness, Radio Systems Corporation, Knoxville, TN, USA or a Zack and Zoey Nylon Pet Harness, Pet Any Way LLC, model US2395 14 99). We walked each dog to a grassy field (16.6 ha; 42°28′20″ N, 76°26′22″ W) across the street from the shelter.

We allowed dogs to set the pace of walks and scored their behavior during the first 20 min of the walk. We recorded each urination and whether the urination was preceded by sniffing (dog stopped walking and investigated with its nose either a location on the ground or an obvious target in the environment, such as a mound of vegetation, tree trunk, signpost, bench, or fence surrounding the outdoor enclosure). We also recorded whether the urination was directed at either the location sniffed or a target (within 20 cm; Ranson and Beach, 1985). Thus, the following three situations would be classified as a directed urination: 1) dog sniffed a location on the ground and then urinated on that location; 2) dog sniffed a target and then urinated on that target; and 3) dog directed urine at a target without first sniffing the target. Some authors consider all urinations as scent marking events in canids (Gese and Ruff, 1997). Others stipulate that the urination must be directed at a target to qualify as scent marking and consider that urinations without a directional quality are simple eliminations (Kleiman, 1966). Given this difference in opinion, we recorded all urinations (consistent with the broad definition of scent marking) and whether each was directed at a target (in line with the narrower definition of scent marking; this definition would exclude urinations on the ground which were not preceded by sniffing the particular location, so-called simple eliminations). Finally, we recorded each defecation. Most often we collected behavioral data using a check sheet. On occasion, BM verbally recorded observations using the voice memo app on an iPhone 5 (model ME306LL/A, Apple Inc., Cupertino, CA, USA) and later transferred these data to a check sheet within a few hours of the walk.

Dogs were adopted throughout our study, so number of walks per dog varied, ranging from 1 to 13 (1 walk, 164 dogs total, 33 small, 56 medium, 75 large; 2–3 walks, 69 dogs total, 21 small, 24 medium, 24 large; 4–5 walks, 23 dogs total, 6 small, 5 medium, 12 large; 6–7 walks, 18 dogs total, 3 small, 4 medium, 11 large; 8–13 walks, 7 dogs total, 2 small, 2 medium, 3 large). Of the 117 dogs walked multiple times, they fell into size classes as follows: small, 32/117 (27.4%); medium, 35/117 (29.9%); large, 50/117 (42.7%). These values are very similar to the overall population of 281 dogs walked: small, 65/281 (23.1%); medium, 91/281 (32.4%); large, 125/281 (44.5%). Thus, no size class was overrepresented in the dogs walked multiple times. Repeat walks of a given dog always occurred on different days. We scored scent-marking behavior on a total of 619 walks. Most dogs were spayed or neutered at the time of observation: of the 158 males walked, 136 (86.1%) were neutered prior to their first walk and of the 123 females walked, 104 (84.6%) were spayed prior to their first walk. Forty-one dogs (22 males and 19 females) were intact at the time of their first walk. Of these 41 dogs, 20 were walked more than once and 18 of these dogs (4 small, 8 medium, and 6 large) were neutered or spayed before their second or third walk (the remaining two dogs were intact for both of their walks). Females re-entered the study 2–12 days after surgery and males re-entered 1–4 days after surgery; variation within sex in days to re-entry reflect availability of dogs (e.g., volunteers might have walked a dog, so we could not on a given day), not health issues associated with surgery. Existing data indicate that neither spaying nor neutering adult dogs influences their urinary behavior (frequency and posture of males, Beach, 1974; propensity of males and females to raise a hindlimb when urinating, Gough and McGuire, 2015; latency of males to mark and number of marks, Hart, 1974; likelihood of countermarking by males and females, Lisberg and Snowdon, 2011; frequency and percent directed urinations of females, Wirant and McGuire, 2004), so we saw no reason to restrict our data to one reproductive state (e.g., spayed/neutered). According to shelter personnel who monitored health and behavior of the dogs, intact females were not in either proestrus or estrus at the time of our walks.

We photographed each dog at the end of the first walk and measured height at withers (cm). We also collected the following information from shelter records: name, identification number, intake date, sex, age, body mass (kg), and whether the dog was intact or spayed/neutered. We used intake date to calculate number of days that dogs had been at the shelter at the time of their walk (=time at shelter; median, 20 days; range, 3–227 days; 75% of walks occurred within 1 month after arrival at the shelter). Nineteen dogs were adopted and returned to the shelter after periods of time ranging from a few days to several months; we did not include time at shelter for these dogs after their return. We carried out all procedures under protocol 2012-0150, which was approved by Cornell University's Institutional Animal Care and Use Committee.

2.3. Statistical analyses

We used linear mixed effects models to analyze rate of urination per min (total number of urinations/20 min) and percent of urinations that were directed (number of directed urinations/total number of urinations × 100). Almost all dogs urinated at least once during a walk: only three males (two large and one small) and three females (two large and one medium) did not urinate. We included data from these six dogs in our analysis of rate of urination. Some dogs did not defecate during a walk. For those that did, number of defecations showed little variation (typically 1; range, 1–3). Additionally, when considering the 400 walks during which defecation occurred, numbers of defecations were as follows: one (82% of walks); two (15% of walks); and three (3%). Thus, rather than analyzing rate of defecation, we used logistic regression to determine significant predictors of defecating during a walk. The models for rate of urination per min, percent of directed urinations, and likelihood of defecating at least once during a walk included dog as a random factor and the following fixed factors: size class, sex, time at shelter, and a size class by sex interaction. The size class by sex interaction was not significant for any of the three models,

Table 1
Descriptive statistics (Mean ± SD; number of walks; range) for rate of urination per min and percent of directed urinations. Percentages of walks in which dogs defecated also are shown.

	Rate of urination[a]	% Directed urinations[b]	% Walks with defecation[c]
Male			
Small	0.62 ± 0.52; 81; 0.00–2.10	92.9 ± 21.9; 80; 0–100	72.8 (59/81)
Medium	0.34 ± 0.23; 72; 0.05–1.05	85.0 ± 31.9; 72; 0–100	62.5 (45/72)
Large	0.37 ± 0.22; 197; 0.00–1.10	87.1 ± 27.6; 193; 0–100	64.0 (126/197)
Female			
Small	0.21 ± 0.16; 68; 0.05–0.70	51.3 ± 41.3; 68; 0–100	66.2 (45/68)
Medium	0.16 ± 0.11; 108; 0.00–0.55	51.2 ± 39.7; 107; 0–100	68.5 (74/108)
Large	0.18 ± 0.15; 93; 0.00–0.70	48.5 ± 38.8; 91; 0–100	54.8 (51/93)
Total dogs			
Small	0.44 ± 0.45; 149; 0.00–2.10	73.8 ± 38.3; 148; 0–100	69.8 (104/149)
Medium	0.24 ± 0.19; 180; 0.00–1.05	64.8 ± 40.2; 179; 0–100	66.1 (119/180)
Large	0.31 ± 0.22; 290; 0.00–1.10	74.8 ± 36.4; 284; 0–100	61.0 (177/290)

[a] Total number of urinations/20 min.
[b] Number of directed urinations/total number of urinations × 100.
[c] Number of walks with at least one defecation/total number of walks.

so we removed the interaction from each. Contrasts were carried out with P values adjusted for number of contrasts using the Tukey method. We analyzed data using either JMP Pro 12 (2015. SAS Institute, Cary, NC, USA) or R, version 3.0.3 (R Foundation for Statistical Computing, Vienna, Austria).

3. Results

Descriptive statistics for the three dependent variables are shown in Table 1. The statistics in Table 1 consider each of the 619 walks as independent, and are meant to provide a general overview of the raw data. In contrast, in the analyses described in Sections 3.1 and 3.2, the models included dog as a random factor, so walks within dog were not considered independent.

3.1. Urination

Size class influenced rate of urination per min ($F_{2,303.4} = 6.33$, $P = 0.002$): small dogs urinated at higher rates than both medium and large dogs, which did not differ from one another (Table 2). Sex also influenced rate of urination per min ($F_{1,306.8} = 71.05$, $P < 0.0001$), with males urinating at higher rates than females (Table 2). Time at shelter positively influenced rate of urination ($F_{1,502.9} = 12.23$, $P = 0.0005$): with each additional day at the shelter, rate of urination per min increased by 0.0011 (Table 2).

There was a tendency for size class to influence percent of directed urinations ($F_{2,267} = 2.89$, $P = 0.057$): small dogs directed more of their urinations than large dogs (Table 3). Small dogs did not differ from medium dogs with respect to percent of directed urinations, and medium and large dogs did not differ from one another (Table 3). Sex influenced percent of directed urinations ($F_{1,269.6} = 112.27$, $P < 0.0001$), with males directing more of their urinations than females (Table 3). Time at shelter positively influenced percent of directed urinations ($F_{1,483.3} = 7.80$, $P = 0.005$): with each additional day at the shelter, percent of directed urinations increased by 0.135 (Table 3).

3.2. Defecation

The logistic regression analysis revealed a tendency for small dogs to be more likely than large dogs to defecate during a walk ($P = 0.06$; Table 4). However, none of the contrasts performed on least square means was significant. Sex was not a significant predictor of defecation during a walk ($P = 0.62$; Table 4). Time at shelter was a significant predictor of defecation during a walk ($P = 0.006$): with each additional day, the odds of defecation increased by 2% (Table 4).

4. Discussion

Body size influenced urinary behavior of shelter dogs during walks on a leash. Consistent with our prediction, small dogs urinated at higher rates than both medium and large dogs. Small dogs

Table 2
Effects of sex, size class, and time at shelter on rate of urination per min by dogs during a 20-min walk.

Parameter	LS Means (95% CI)	β	SE β	df	t	P
Intercept		0.448	0.030	310.6	14.84	<0.0001
Small[a]	0.36 (0.31–0.42)					
Medium	0.26 (0.22–0.31)	−0.099	0.037	292.8	−2.72	0.007
Large	0.24 (0.21–0.29)	−0.118	0.034	293.5	−3.48	0.0006
Male[b]	0.41 (0.37–0.44)					
Female	0.18 (0.14–0.22)	−0.231	0.027	306.8	−8.43	<0.0001
Time at shelter		0.0011	0.0003	502.9	3.50	0.0005

[a] Small is the reference.
[b] Male is the reference.

Table 3
Effects of sex, size class, and time at shelter on percent of directed urinations (number of directed urinations/total number of urinations × 100) by dogs during a 20-min walk.

Parameter	LS Means (95% CI)	β	SE β	df	t	P
Intercept		89.324	4.381	275.0	20.39	<0.0001
Small[a]	71.8 (63.9–79.8)					
Medium	65.6 (58.8–72.5)	−6.200	5.315	256.9	−1.17	0.24
Large	60.0 (54.1–66.0)	−11.810	4.961	257.9	−2.38	0.02
Male[b]	87.0 (81.7–92.4)					
Female	44.6 (38.7–50.6)	−42.393	4.001	269.6	−10.60	<0.0001
Time at shelter		0.135	0.048	483.3	2.79	0.005

[a] Small is the reference.
[b] Male is the reference.

Table 4
Effects of size class, sex, and time at shelter on probability of defecation by dogs during a 20-min walk.

Parameter	LS Means (95% CI)	β	SE β	Z	P	Odds ratio
Intercept		0.888	0.424	2.10	0.04	NA
Small[a]	0.79 (0.64–0.89)					
Medium	0.69 (0.55–0.81)	−0.511	0.482	−1.06	0.29	0.60
Large	0.61 (0.48–0.73)	−0.867	0.454	−1.91	0.06	0.42
Male[b]	0.72 (0.61–0.81)					
Female	0.68 (0.56–0.79)	−0.176	0.361	−0.49	0.62	0.84
Time at shelter		0.019	0.007	2.77	0.006	1.02

[a] Small is the reference.
[b] Male is the reference.

also directed more of their urinations at targets in the environment than did large dogs. Small dogs did not differ from medium dogs in percent directed urinations (71.8% versus 65.6%, respectively), although the general pattern was consistent with our prediction that small dogs would be more likely to communicate via scent marking than larger dogs. As predicted, males urinated at higher rates and directed more of their urinations than females, and likelihood of defecating during a walk did not significantly differ between size classes or sexes. In contrast to our prediction that rate of urination, percent of directed urinations, and likelihood of defecation would not vary in relation to time spent at this shelter, we found that time at shelter positively influenced all three behavioral measures.

Our findings that rate of urination and percentage of directed urinations during walks were higher in small dogs than large dogs are consistent with those of McGreevy et al. (2013) who surveyed dog owners about problematic in-home behaviors associated with urination. These authors reported that urination when left alone, urine marking, and emotional urination were more common in smaller dogs (height used as a measure of body size). McGreevy et al. (2013) also reported that defecation when left home alone was more common in smaller dogs. In our study, the probability of defecating during a walk was higher in small dogs (0.79) than large dogs (0.61), but the difference failed to reach statistical significance. Most dogs do not scent mark via defecation (Cafazzo et al., 2012; McGuire, 2016; Sprague and Anisko, 1973), so we did not expect major differences in likelihood of defecation between small dogs and large dogs.

McGreevy et al. (2013) suggested several potential explanations for their overall finding that problematic behaviors, eliminatory and otherwise, were more common or pronounced in dogs as height decreases: 1) selection against problematic behaviors may be relaxed in small dogs because owners might be more tolerant of these behaviors in small dogs than large dogs; 2) characteristics of the environments in which small dogs are kept may induce problematic behaviors; 3) selection for small body size may be associated with neurological changes that make small dogs more reactive than large dogs; and 4) artificial selection for infantile behavior in small dogs. We suggest a new adaptive explanation for differences in urinary behavior between small and large dogs: small dogs favor urine marking over direct social interactions because direct interactions may be particularly risky for them. Two studies provide support for the suggestion that small dogs avoid direct interactions with other dogs. First, Leaver and Reimchen (2008) used a life-size model of a Labrador retriever to examine the effect of domestic dog tail length and motion on the behavior of off-leash dogs. They found that dogs smaller than the model displayed lower motivation to approach and interact with the model than dogs larger than the model. Second, Taylor et al. (2010) examined behavioral responses of small, medium, and large dogs to playbacks of growls manipulated to correspond to a dog either smaller or larger than themselves. Large dogs were more motivated to investigate playback stimuli when growls simulated a smaller intruder. Small dogs responded less than medium and large dogs to both playback conditions. Leaver and Reimchen (2008) and Taylor et al. (2010) suggested the behavior of small dogs in their studies reflects reluctance to engage in potentially costly direct social interactions. We further suggest that small dogs preferentially communicate via the more indirect route of marking with urine.

An alternative explanation exists for our finding that small dogs urinated at higher rates than both medium and large dogs. Instead of the higher rates by small dogs representing a preference for communicating via scent marking over direct interaction, the rates could reflect the known relationship between bladder capacity and body size: bladder capacity increases with body mass in mammals (Yang et al., 2014). Thus, the higher rate of urination by small dogs could be due to small dogs having smaller bladders than medium and large dogs. However, factors other than bladder capacity must influence rate of urination as evidenced by the consistent sex difference within each size class in our study: on average, rates of urination for males were at least twice those of females, and this pattern characterized small, medium, and large dogs (Table 1). Additionally, bladder capacity cannot explain why, when compared with large dogs, small dogs also directed more of their urinations at targets in the environment.

We found that males urinated at higher rates and directed more of their urinations at targets than did females; these findings are consistent with previous reports of sex differences in the urinary behavior of mature dogs (Beach, 1974; Bekoff, 1979; Lisberg and Snowdon, 2011; Martins and Valle, 1948; Sprague and Anisko, 1973). Sex differences did not characterize likelihood of defecation in our study. Similarly, Sprague and Anisko (1973) found no difference in the percentage of 3-min tests that were positive for defecation when male and female laboratory beagles were individually placed in an outdoor enclosure: males defecated in 19% of tests and females in 17% of tests. In our study, we expected to find sex differences in urinary behavior, but not in likelihood of defecation because these patterns are consistent with results from analyses of first walks of many of these dogs (McGuire, 2016). In other members of Canidae, sex differences in urinary behavior have been reported during certain seasons for some species and particular individuals (red foxes, Fawcett et al., 2013; gray wolves, members of dominant breeding pair, Peterson et al., 2002), with males urinating more frequently than females. Rates of urination and defecation did not vary by sex in coyotes (Gese and Ruff, 1997).

In our study, time spent at the shelter positively influenced rate of urination, percent of directed urinations, and likelihood of defecation during a walk. Time spent at the shelter did not significantly influence these three categories of behavior during first walks of dogs at this shelter (McGuire, 2016); thus, we interpret the positive influence of time at shelter in the present study as resulting from our inclusion of multiple walks on individual dogs. A positive influence of time spent at the shelter on behavior could reflect dogs becoming more familiar with their surroundings and routine, as well as with us. Behavioral and physiological data indicate that dogs are initially stressed by shelter life but that most adjust over a period of days or a few weeks. Wells and Hepper (1992) examined behavioral responses of dogs on their 1st, 3rd, and 5th days of living in a shelter, and found that as time spent at the shelter increased, dogs ate more rapidly and were less agitated and more relaxed in the presence of an unfamiliar person looking into their cage; time spent at the shelter did not influence the response of dogs to a novel object in their cage. Dogs exhibit elevated levels of cortisol, which indicates a stress response, for their first few days to 2 weeks in a shelter, with levels declining thereafter (Hennessy et al., 1997, 2001; Stephen and Ledger, 2006). If the changes in behavior that we observed with increasing time spent at the Tompkins County SPCA simply reflected the dogs' increasing familiarity with their surroundings and routine, then we would expect such changes to be apparent on our first walks of dogs kept at this shelter for varying periods of time, but they were not (McGuire, 2016). The positive effects of time at shelter on rate of urination, percent of directed urinations, and likelihood of defecation only became apparent when we included multiple walks on individual dogs; this suggests that increasing familiarity with us as walkers was the key driver of these behavioral changes in the dogs. Shelter dogs rapidly form attachments with humans who interact with them (Gácsi et al., 2001), so it is possible that with each walk the dogs in our study became increasingly familiar with us and more comfortable displaying scent-marking behavior. The challenging conditions of shelter life have been suggested to influence urinary posture in dogs (Gough and McGuire, 2015) and likely influence other eliminatory behaviors as well.

Our study had two limitations related to the environment in which we walked dogs. First, we were unable to control for the number of obvious targets each dog encountered during the walk (e.g., there were variations in the specific routes taken, depending on where the dog wanted to go, presence of other dogs, activities in the fields, such as mowing, etc.). Second, we could not control whether other dogs had previously been walked by volunteers or staff on the same route; such control was impossible in our research setting and would be difficult in any outdoor area. We previously showed that scent-marking behavior of dogs is robust to very different environmental conditions. For example, despite a large difference in the area available for walking at the two shelters at which we study dogs (16.6 ha at the Tompkins shelter versus 0.3 ha at the Cortland shelter) and likely differences in number of available targets and number of scents left by previous dogs, we have found the same sex and age differences in marking behaviors and relationships between marking behaviors at the two shelters (McGuire, 2016). Environmental differences between the two shelters are likely more dramatic than those between different walking routes at the Tompkins shelter, so we expect our findings regarding body size to be robust to environmental conditions encountered on different routes at the Tompkins shelter.

5. Conclusions

Using domestic dogs that have extreme variation in body size, we have shown that small dogs scent mark more frequently than do large dogs. This pattern is just the opposite of what would be expected if characteristics of scent marking reflected competitive ability, as has been shown for some mammals: competitive ability, for which body size can serve as a proxy, is positively correlated with frequency of marking, density of marks, and rate at which marks are refreshed (Gosling and Roberts, 2001; Hurst and Beynon, 2004; Johnson, 1973). We suggest that small dogs preferentially communicate via scent marking because of the indirect nature of this mode of communication, which allows them to avoid costly direct interactions. In mammals, body size is known to affect auditory (Fitch and Hauser, 2003) and visual communication (Moynihan, 1967). Our data on dogs, together with the findings regarding body size and scent marking in dwarf mongooses (Sharpe et al., 2012) and house mice (Gosling et al., 2000), show that body size can affect chemical communication as well. Problematic in-home behaviors are more common in small dogs than large dogs (McGreevy et al., 2013). Our findings for urination and defecation by dogs during walks provide context for interpreting these size-based differences.

Acknowledgments

We thank Nancy Given and her clients for making possible our collection of pilot data on their dogs; this allowed us to fine-tune our methods for subsequent work with shelter dogs. Jim Bouderau, Executive Director of the Tompkins County SPCA, gave us permission to study dogs at the shelter, and staff and volunteers provided background information on dogs. Stephen Parry provided statistical advice and William E. Bemis, Nancy G. Solomon, Brian Keane, and Malory Owen read an earlier version of this manuscript. Finally, we thank Andrea Cerruti, Claudia Gerecke, Will Gough, Boomer Olsen, Cassandra Ramirez, Renee Staffeld, and Giuseppe Tumminello for assistance with walking dogs and data collection.

References

Archer, J., 1988. The Behavioural Biology of Aggression. Cambridge University Press, New York, pp. 166–171.
Beach, F.A., 1974. Effects of gonadal hormones on urinary behavior in dogs. Physiol. Behav. 12, 1005–1013, http://dx.doi.org/10.1016/0031-9384(74)90148-6.
Bekoff, M., 1979. Scent-marking by free-ranging domestic dogs – olfactory and visual components. Biol. Behav. 4, 123–139.
Biben, M., 1982. Urine-marking during agonistic encounters in the bush dog (Speothos venaticus). Zoo Biol. 1, 359–362, http://dx.doi.org/10.1002/zoo.1430010409.
Bollen, K.S., Horowitz, J., 2008. Behavioral evaluation and demographic information in the assessment of aggressiveness in shelter dogs. Appl. Anim. Behav. Sci. 112, 120–135, http://dx.doi.org/10.1016/j.applanim.2007.07.007.
Cafazzo, S., Natoli, E., Valsecchi, P., 2012. Scent-marking behaviour in a pack of free-ranging domestic dogs. Ethology 118, 955–966, http://dx.doi.org/10.1111/j.1439-0310.2012.02088.x.
Fawcett, J.K., Fawcett, J.M., Soulsbury, C.D., 2013. Seasonal and sex differences in urine marking rates of wild red foxes Vulpes vulpes. J. Ethol. 31, 41–47, http://dx.doi.org/10.1007/s10164-012-0348-7.
Fitch, W.T., Hauser, M.D., 2003. Unpacking 'honesty': vertebrate vocal production and the evolution of acoustic signals. In: Simmons, A.M., Fay, R.R., Popper, A.N. (Eds.), Acoustic Communication. Springer, New York, pp. 65–137.
Gácsi, M., Topál, J., Miklósi, Á., Dóka, A., Csányi, V., 2001. Attachment behavior of adult dogs (Canis familiaris) living at rescue centers: forming new bonds. J. Comp. Psychol. 115, 423–431, http://dx.doi.org/10.1037//0735-7036.113.4.423.
Gese, E.M., Ruff, R.L., 1997. Scent-marking by coyotes, Canis latrans: the influence of social and ecological factors. Anim. Behav. 54, 1155–1166, http://dx.doi.org/10.1006/anbe.1997.0561.
Gosling, L.M., Roberts, S.C., 2001. Scent-marking by male mammals: cheat-proof signals to competitors and mates. Adv. Stud. Behav. 30, 169–217, http://dx.doi.org/10.1016/S0065-3454(01)80007-3.
Gosling, L.M., Roberts, S.C., Thornton, E.A., Andrew, M.J., 2000. Life history costs of olfactory status signalling in mice. Behav. Ecol. Sociobiol. 48, 328–332, http://dx.doi.org/10.1007/s002650000242.
Gough, W., McGuire, B., 2015. Urinary posture and motor laterality in dogs (Canis lupus familiaris) at two shelters. Appl. Anim. Behav. Sci. 168, 61–70, http://dx.doi.org/10.1016/j.applanim.2015.04.006.
Harrington, F.H., 1981. Urine-marking and caching behavior in the wolf. Behaviour 76, 280–288, http://dx.doi.org/10.1163/156853981x00112.
Harrington, F.H., 1982. Urine marking at food and caches in captive coyotes. Can. J. Zool. 60, 776–782.
Hart, B.L., 1974. Environmental and hormonal influences on urine marking behavior in the adult male dog. Behav. Biol. 11, 167–176, http://dx.doi.org/10.1139/z82-107.
Hennessy, M.B., Davis, H.N., Williams, M.T., Mellott, C., Douglas, C.W., 1997. Plasma cortisol levels of dogs at a county animal shelter. Physiol. Behav. 62, 485–490, http://dx.doi.org/10.1016/S0031-9384(97)80328-9.
Hennessy, M.B., Voith, V.L., Mazzei, S.J., Buttram, J., Miller, D.D., Linden, F., 2001. Behavior and cortisol levels of dogs in a public animal shelter, and an exploration of the ability of these measures to predict problem behavior after adoption. Appl. Anim. Behav. Sci. 73, 217–233, http://dx.doi.org/10.1016/S0168-1591(01)00139-3.

Henry, J.D., 1977. The use of urine marking in the scavenging behavior of the red fox (*Vulpes vulpes*). Behaviour 61, 82–105, http://dx.doi.org/10.1163/156853977x00496.

Huntingford, F.A., Turner, A.K., 1987. Animal Conflict. Chapman and Hall, London, UK.

Hurst, J.L., Beynon, R.J., 2004. Scent wars: the chemobiology of competitive signalling in mice. BioEssays 26, 1288–1298.

Johnson, R.P., 1973. Scent marking in mammals. Anim. Behav. 21, 521–535.

Kleiman, D., 1966. Scent marking in the Canidae. Symp. Zool. Soc. Lond. 18, 167–177.

Leaver, S.D.A., Reimchen, T.E., 2008. Behavioural responses of *Canis familiaris* to different tail lengths of a remotely-controlled life-size dog replica. Behaviour 145, 377–390, http://dx.doi.org/10.1163/156853908783402894.

Lisberg, A.E., Snowdon, C.T., 2011. Effects of sex, social status and gonadectomy on countermarking by domestic dogs, *Canis familiaris*. Anim. Behav. 81, 757–764, http://dx.doi.org/10.1016/j.anbehav.2011.01.006.

Martins, T., Valle, J.R., 1948. Hormonal regulation of the micturition behavior of the dog. J. Comp. Physiol. Psychol. 41, 301–311.

McGreevy, P.D., Georgevsky, D., Carrasco, J., Valenzuela, M., Duffy, D.L., Serpell, J.A., 2013. Dog behavior co-varies with height, bodyweight and skull shape. PLoS One 8 (12), e80529, http://dx.doi.org/10.1371/journal.pone.0080529.

McGuire, B., 2016. Scent marking in shelter dogs: effects of sex and age. Appl. Anim. Behav. Sci. 182, 15–22, http://dx.doi.org/10.1016/j.applanim.2016.06.001.

Moynihan, M., 1967. Comparative aspects of communication in New World primates. In: Morris, D. (Ed.), Primate Ethology. Weidenfeld and Nicolson, London, UK, pp. 236–266.

Pal, S.K., 2003. Urine marking by free-ranging dogs (*Canis familiaris*) in relation to sex, season, place and posture. Appl. Anim. Behav. Sci. 80, 45–59, http://dx.doi.org/10.1016/S0168-1591(02)00178-8.

Peters, R.P., Mech, L.D., 1975. Scent-marking in wolves. Am. Sci. 63, 628–637.

Peterson, R.O., Jacobs, A.K., Drummer, T.D., Mech, L.D., Smith, D.W., 2002. Leadership behavior in relation to dominance and reproductive status in gray wolves, *Canis lupus*. Can. J. Zool. 80, 1405–1412, http://dx.doi.org/10.1139/z02-124.

Porton, I., 1983. Bush dog urine-marking: its role in pair formation and maintenance. Anim. Behav. 31, 1061–1069, http://dx.doi.org/10.1016/S0003-3472(83)80013-X.

Ranson, E., Beach, F.A., 1985. Effects of testosterone on ontogeny of urinary behavior in male and female dogs. Horm. Behav. 19, 36–51, http://dx.doi.org/10.1016/0018-506X(85)90004-2.

Řezáč, P., Viziová, P., Dobešová, M., Havlíček, Z., Pospíšilová, D., 2011. Factors affecting dog–dog interactions on walks with their owners. Appl. Anim. Behav. Sci. 134, 170–176, http://dx.doi.org/10.1016/j.applanim.2011.08.006.

Rothman, R.J., Mech, L.D., 1979. Scent-marking in lone wolves and newly formed pairs. Anim. Behav. 27, 750–760, http://dx.doi.org/10.1016/0003-3472(79)90010-1.

Sharpe, L.L., 2015. Handstand scent marking: height matters to dwarf mongooses. Anim. Behav. 105, 173–179, http://dx.doi.org/10.1016/j.anbehav.2015.04.019.

Sharpe, L.L., Jooste, M.M., Cherry, M.I., 2012. Handstand scent marking in the dwarf mongoose (*Helogale parvula*). Ethology 118, 575–583, http://dx.doi.org/10.1111/j.1439-0310.2012.02045.x.

Sprague, R.H., Anisko, J.J., 1973. Elimination patterns in the laboratory beagle. Behaviour 47, 257–267, http://dx.doi.org/10.1163/156853973x00102.

Stephen, J.M., Ledger, R.A., 2006. A longitudinal evaluation of urinary cortisol in kennelled dogs, *Canis familiaris*. Physiol. Behav. 87, 911–916, http://dx.doi.org/10.1016/j.physbeh.2006.02.015.

Sternberg, S., 2006. Assess-A-Pet: The Manual. Assess-A-Pet, New York.

Taylor, A.M., Reby, D., McComb, K., 2010. Size communication in domestic dog, *Canis familiaris*, growls. Anim. Behav. 79, 205–210, http://dx.doi.org/10.1016/j.anbehav.2009.10.030.

Wells, D., Hepper, P.G., 1992. The behaviour of dogs in a rescue shelter. Anim. Welf. 1, 171–186.

Wirant, S.C., McGuire, B., 2004. Urinary behavior of female domestic dogs (*Canis familiaris*): influence of reproductive condition, location, and age. Appl. Anim. Behav. Sci. 85, 335–348, http://dx.doi.org/10.1016/j.applanim.2003.09.012.

Wirant, S.C., Halvorsen, K., McGuire, B., 2007. Preliminary observations on the urinary behaviour of female Jack Russell Terriers in relation to stage of the oestrous cycle, location, and age. Appl. Anim. Behav. Sci. 106, 161–166, http://dx.doi.org/10.1016/j.applanim.2006.07.005.

Yang, P.J., Pham, J., Choo, J., Hu, D.L., 2014. Duration of urination does not change with body size. Proc. Nat. Acad. Sci. 111, 11932–11937, http://dx.doi.org/10.1073/pnas.1402289111.

	Outline
Introduction	**Issue**: scent marking & _____ Established findings: a _____ relationship between competitive ability and scent marking **The purpose of the present study** Hypothesis: Does scent marking behavior of mammals _____ _____ ?

Material and methods	**Material**
	1. **Dogs**
	  • Types
	  • Age
	2. **Care and housing**
	  • Behavior examination
	  • Housing: _____
	  • Feeding
	Methods
	1. **Experimental procedures**
	  • Urination & _____
	  • Devices:
	    ■ A check sheet
	    ■ _____ app
	    ■ iPhone
	  • Size classification
	    ■ Photograph
	  • Shelter records info
	2. **Statistical analyses**
	  • _____ models
	  • Statistics type:
	    1. Number of _____ per min
	    2. Percent of urinations directed at _____
	    3. Number of walks with _____

Results	1. **Urination**
	  • _____ influenced rate of urination per min
	  • There was a tendency for _____ _____.
	2. **Defecation**
	  • There was a tendency for small dogs _____ _____ during a walk.

continued

	Outline

Discussion	**Summary of findings**
	• Body size _____
	  ■ The rate of urination and percentage of directed urinations during walks were _____.
	  ■ Small dogs also directed more of their urinations at _____ in the environment.
	  ■ _____ positively influenced the behavioral measures.
	Explanations
	• From McGreevy et al.
	• From the authors
	  ■ Body size _____.
	  Reason: Direct interactions may be particularly _____ for small dogs.
	  ■ Positive influence of time at the rate of urination, percent of directed urinations, and defecation
	  Reason: _____ on individual dogs
	Limitations
	• Not able to control the _____
	• Could not control whether _____

Conclusions	**Conclusions** • Small dogs preferentially communicate via _____ because of the indirect nature. • Body size can affect _____. • Problematic in-home behaviors are _____ in small dogs than large dogs. **Significance of the study** • The study provides the context for interpreting _____.

❷ Scan the paper "Scent marking in shelter dogs: effects of body size" and find examples of the following features this textbook covers.

(1) Definition

(2) Phrases showing cause and effect

(3) Synonyms for "scent marking"

(4) Tentative or cautious language (hedging)

(5) Citations (reported speech)

(6) Reporting words

(7) Narration

    ① Which part of the paper is typical narration?

② Which point of view is used?

③ Is the narration objective or subjective? What makes it objective or subjective?

(8) Description

① Find a description paragraph in the paper.

② What is described? What details are used?

③ How are the details organized?

(9) Explanation

① Find an expository paragraph in the paper.

② What expository methods are used?

Comparison

Compare the language features of "Is your dog lying to other dogs about its size?" and "Scent marking in shelter dogs: effects of body size" from the following aspects, and give a summary of their features.

	Is your dog lying to other dogs about its size?	Comment	Scent marking in shelter dogs: effects of body size	Comment
Point of view				
Reporting words				
Direct/Indirect speech				
Use of definition				
Active voice/ Passive voice				
Words				
Summary				

English Reading and Writing for Academic Purposes

Lesson 1
"Call for papers" announcement

Overview

☑ Reading

- "Call for papers" announcement
- Function, style & content

☑ Vocabulary

- Academic words: Words for announcements

Reading

❶ **Discuss these questions with your partner.**
1. Have you ever received "Call for papers"?
2. What is the function of "Call for papers"?
3. What is the style of "Call for papers"?
4. What contents are usually included in "Call for papers"?

❷ **Read the following paragraphs and check your answers to the previous questions.**

"Call for papers" is a notice or an announcement published by a conference or a journal. It functions as a public or official statement that gives people information about paper calling. Though a notice or an announcement can be written or oral in form, "Call for papers" is usually written and published in magazines or on websites due to its formal and official context.

Normally, "Call for papers" consists of three parts—the title, the body and the signature. The title summarizes the most important information in a very brief way. The body consists of the detailed information on the title. The signature leaves the announcement publisher's contact information, including the conference/journal's name, email box, telephone number, etc.

❸ **The following words and expressions often occur in "Call for papers" announcements. Guess their meanings and then match the words with their meanings on the right.**

1. symposium   A. a time or date before which a participant should make an official record of a conference or an activity
2. proceedings   B. written records of presented papers and discussions at a meeting or conference
3. registration deadline   C. complete paper is expected to be submitted at a time before ...
4. full text due on ...   D. a kind of meeting, but exclusively for specialized academic discussion
5. template   E. add something to a list of ...
6. issues and areas   F. a model on which submitted papers should be based
7. index   G. official notice of allowing a paper to be presented on a conference

8. acceptance notification   H. topics of discussion

❹ **Read the sample announcements and answer the questions that follow.**

> **Sample 1**
>
> **13th Conference on Man-Machine-Environment**
> **System Engineering Call for Papers**
>
> The 13th Conference on Man-Machine-Environment System Engineering will take place in Yantai, China, October 2013. The Conference Sponsor is the Man-Machine-Environment System Engineering Committee of China. Cosponsor is Scientific Research Publishing (SCIRP), USA. (Please see the web www.mmese.com)
>
> **CONFERENCE THEMES**
>
> The Conference is designed to bring participants up to date on the MMESE theory and applications.
>
> Since MMESE involves seven relations (see the right figure), the Conference will cover the following topics, but not limit to:
>
> (1) Research on Man Character (M)
>
> (2) Research on Machine Character (M)
>
> (3) Research on Environment Character (E)
>
> (4) Research on Man-Machine Relationship (MMR)
>
> (5) Research on Man-Environment Relationship (MER)
>
> (6) Research on Machine-Environment Relationship (MER)
>
> (7) Research on overall performance of Man-Machine-Environment System (MMES)
>
> (8) Applications research of MMESE
>
> **SUBMISSION INSTRUCTIONS**
>
> **A. Style for paper**
>
> Papers written in English or Chinese will be considered. Papers are generally no more than 4 pages in length (including Figures and Tables). Papers should be written in double-column format.
>
> **B. Preparation for paper**
>
> The paper should contain the following information:
>
> (1) Article title and subtitle
>
> (2) Name of each author (first initials followed by last name) and the author's primary institution, city, and country
>
> (3) Abstract of no more than 150 words
>
> (4) Several keywords for indexing purposes (exclude words that already appear in the title/subtitle)

> (5) Text
>> (a) Level 1 text headings should appear in solid caps, centered; Level 2 headings are lowercase bold caps, flush to the left margin; Level 3 headings are in italics, flush to the left margin.
>> (b) In the text, each figure (photos, graphs, line drawings) should be high resolution. Do not use shading as background or to indicate differences in quantity (e. g. as sometimes appears in bar graphs); instead, use patterns such as horizontal, vertical, diagonal, and zigzag lines. Line weight should be at least 1 point. Do not use color figures.
>> (c) Magnitudes of all measured quantities must be given in the International System of Units.
> (6) References should appear in a separate section at the end of the paper, with items referred to by numerals in square brackets. References must be complete:
>> (a) Style for papers: author (first initials followed by last name), title in quotations, periodical, volume, initial and final page number, month, year.
>> (b) Style for books: author, title, location, publisher, year, chapter, initial and final page number.
>
> **C. Submission for paper**
>
> For safety, all submissions for paper should send by e-mail to the following address: mmese@ sina. com. A receipt will be sent to the author by e-mail.
>
> **Important Note**
>
> All notifications and correspondence concerning your submission are sent to you by e-mail. If your e-mail address changes, be sure to notify the Conference.
>
> **PUBLICATIONS**
>
> The Conference proceedings will be published by Scientific Research Publishing (SCIRP), USA. The proceedings will be sent to the ISTP.
>
> **IMPORTANT DATES**
>
> Paper submission: February 28, 2013   Notification of acceptance: March 30, 2013
>
> Modified paper submission: April 30, 2013   Notification of conference: August 30, 2013

1. Is this announcement formal or informal in style? Why do you think so?

2. What is the title of the announcement?

3. What conference is to be held? When and where will it be held?

4. Who are the sponsors of the conference? And who are the organizers?

5. Whom should the paper be submitted to if you are planning to submit a paper, and when?

6. How do you inquire for more details?

Sample 2

Call for Papers—Feature Topic, Vol. 17, No. 3, 2020

Enabling Technologies for Agile Maritime Communication Networks

With the rapid development of maritime activities, there has been a growing demand for high data rate and ultra-reliable maritime communications. Traditionally, this is provided by maritime satellites. Besides, shore and island-based base stations (BSs) can be built to extend the coverage of terrestrial networks providing the fourth-generation (4G) or even the fifth-generation (5G) services. Unmanned aerial vehicles (UAVs)-aided and ship-borne BSs can also be exploited to serve as relaying nodes in maritime mesh/ad-hoc networks. Despite all these approaches, there are still open issues towards the establishment of an agile maritime communication network (MCN). Different from terrestrial communications for urban or suburban coverage, the MCN faces several challenges due to the complicated electromagnetic propagation environment, the limited geometrically available BS sites, and rigorous service demands from mission-critical applications. To address all these challenges, conventional communications and networking theories and methods need to be tailored for maritime application scenarios or new ones should be explored.

The goal of this feature topic is to present the state-of-the-art original research, and the latest advances and innovations in key theories, technologies, and innovative applications for agile MCNs, as well as identify emerging research topics and point out the future research directions. Extended versions of papers published in conferences, symposiums, or workshop proceedings are encouraged for consideration.

SCHEDULE

Submission deadline: October 5, 2019

Acceptance notification (1st round): December 1, 2019

Minor revision due: December 21, 2019

Final decision due: January 5, 2020

Final manuscript due: January 11, 2020

Publication date: March 15, 2020

GUEST EDITORS

Wei Feng, Tsinghua University, China

Bin Lin, Dalian Maritime University, China

Yunfei Chen, University of Warwick, UK

Cheng-xiang Wang, Southeast University, China

Shengming Jiang, Shanghai Maritime University, China

Yuguang Fang, University of Florida, USA

Topics include (but not limited to):
· Hybrid satellite-terrestrial network architecture for MCNs
· Internet of Vessels (IoV) and E-Navigation for smart ocean
· VDES-based broadband communications and intelligent shipping
· Coverage performance analysis and enhancing technologies for MCNs
· UAVs-enabled agile coverage for MCNs
· Broadband communication and networking technologies for Maritime Autonomous Surface Ships (MASS). Routing methods and protocols for maritime mesh/ad-hoc networks
· Measurements and modeling for maritime channels
· Smart channel estimation and adaptive transmission technologies for MCNs
· Radio resource management and optimization for MCNs
· Interference analysis, alignment, avoidance, and coordination in MCNs
· Quality-of-service guaranteeing technologies for MCNs
· Analysis and application of cognitive radio technologies in MCNs
· Physical layer security issues in MCNs
· Mobile edge computing for MCNs
· Advanced non-orthogonal multiple access technologies for MCNs
· Artificial intelligence approaches for agile MCNs
· Hardware testbed or field trial for MCNs

SUBMISSION GUIDELINES

This feature topic "Enabling Technologies for Agile Maritime Communication Networks" invites submissions of original, previously unpublished technical papers and visionary articles exploring the architecture, technologies, and applications in agile MCNs. All submissions will be anonymously peer reviewed and will be evaluated on the basis of their technical merits. Potential topics of interest include, but not limited to areas listed above. Papers should be submitted in two separate .doc files (preferred) or .pdf files: 1) Main document (including paper title, abstract, keywords, and full text); 2) Title page (including paper title, author affiliation, acknowledgement and any other information related to the authors' identification) through the Manuscript Central. Please register or login at http://mc03.manuscriptcentral.com/chinacomm, and then go to the author center and follow the instructions there. Remember to select "Enabling Technologies for Agile Maritime Communication Networks—March Issue 2020" as your manuscript type when submitting; otherwise, it might be considered as a regular paper.
· An abstract of about 150 words
· 3-8 keywords
· Original photographs with high-resolution (300 dpi or greater); eps. ortif. format is preferred; sequentially numbered references.
· Sequentially numbered references. The basic reference format is: author name, article name, issue name (italic), vol., no., page, month, year. For example: Y. M. Huang,

> "pervateture in wireless heterogeneous ...", IEEE *Journal on Selected Areas*, vol. 27, no. 5, pp 34–50, May, 2009.
> - Brief biographies of authors (50–75 words)
> - Contact information, including e-mail and mailing addresses
>
>   Please note that each submission will normally be approximately 4,500 words, with no more than 20 mathematical formulas, accomplished by up to 10 figures and/or tables.

1. What is the title of the announcement?

2. Who makes the announcement?

3. What should the author pay attention to if he/she wants to submit a paper?

Sample 3

8th International Symposium on Teaching English at Tertiary Level

and

17th International Conference of PAAL

Beijing, August 21 – 23, 2012

Jointly organized by

Department of Foreign Languages & Literatures, Tsinghua University, China

Department of English, The Hong Kong Polytechnic University

The Poly U – Tsinghua U Center for Language Sciences

Pan-Pacific Association of Applied Linguistics (PAAL)

Waseda University, Japan

Send submissions to:
E-mail: icte@tsinghua.edu.cn

Important Dates
Deadline for abstract submissions: May 1, 2012
Notice of acceptance: May 20, 2012

Call for Papers
Issues and questions that the symposium will address:
English for academic / specific purposes
Curriculum / Syllabus / Materials development & related research
Computer-based courses
Teaching and assessment

Motivation and leaning strategies

Language policy

Literature and translation studies and teaching

Applied corpus linguistics

Asian Englishes

Your abstract should be a maximum of 250 words. Please include with your abstract: the title of your paper , your name, title, institution, e-mail address, and mailing address.

1. Who are the organizers of the conference?

2. Who are likely to be the participants of the conference?

3. What information is covered in this announcement? Do you need more information if you want to submit a paper? And what is it?

Note:

The conference/journal "Call for papers" announcement usually consists of 3 parts:
- The **Title** is usually "the name of the conference/journal + call for papers";
- The **Body** explains the time, place and purpose of the conference/journal, covered areas or subjects of the conference/journal, requirements on the submitted papers in language, size and format, and means and deadline of abstract or paper submission;
- The **Signature** (lists the name of the conference/journal, the address, the telephone number and QQ number or Wechat account).

Vocabulary

❶ Read the following announcement from ICAIS, and translate the Chinese into English.

Sample 4

征文通知

The 5th International Conference on Artificial Intelligence and Security (ICAIS 2019), formerly called the International Conference on Cloud Computing and Security (ICCCS), will be held during July 26 – 28, 2019 at New York University, New York, USA. The organizing committee is excited to invite you to take part in ICAIS 2019, to discuss issues at the technological frontier of society today as well as interdisciplinary technological trends.

主题涵盖但不限于以下方面：
1. Artificial Intelligence
2. Big Data
3. Cloud Computing and Security
4. Information Hiding
5. IoT Security
6. Multimedia Forensics
7. Encryption and Cyber Security

论文提交注意事项：

All submissions must be in English. This year we are accepting full paper and short paper submissions. Full papers must be at least 12 LNCS pages in length but no more than 15 LNCS pages, including figures and references. Short papers must be 4-7 LNCS pages in length, including figures and references. Authors should refer to the conference submission format to prepare their papers.

The submitted papers must not be previously published anywhere, and must not be submitted to any other conferences before and during the ICAIS 2019 review process. For any accepted paper, at least one author must register and attend the conference to present the paper.

Acceptance:

Manuscripts should present the current research in areas identified in the "call for papers". All submitted manuscripts will be reviewed by experts in the field and will be judged on problem significance, contributions, originality, correctness, technical strength, quality of presentation, relevance, and value to conference attendees.

论文发表相关事宜：

Outstanding papers will be invited for possible publication in SCI-indexed journals. All accepted papers will be published in LNCS and other journals.

大事记：
论文提交截止时间：November 10, 2018
论文录用通知时间：December 1, 2018
注册截止时间：December 17, 2018
影印版论文提交截止时间：December 31, 2018
会议时间：July 26-28, 2019

International Conference on Artificial Intelligence and Security
Tel：+86-(25)-58731244   E-mail：icccsconf@yeah.net
官方微信公众号：1456468

❷ Select the appropriate words or phrases from the box to fill in the blanks of the following announcement, and change the form if necessary.

affiliation	permission	subject
symposium	zip code	include
index	abstract	disposal
invite	sponsored project	keyword
correspondence address	single-blind review	short biography
article title	identity information	reserve all rights
organizing committee	referring period	author school
accepted for publication	declared ahead	author name
notice for revising or publication	call	

Sample 5

_____ for Papers

Business Translation, periodical of SIBT

Business Translation, the quarterly periodical, the first and only scholarly periodical dedicated to business translation studies, is scheduled to launch its inaugural issue at the beginning of 2018.

The periodical is organized by the _____ of the International _____ on Business Translation and Teaching Research (SIBT), co-organized by ENRP Education Technology Co., Ltd, hosted by School of International Business Communications, Dongbei University of Finance & Economics, and published by New Vision Press. It aims to promote the research & teaching of business translation in China and support the professional development and academic exchange of business translators. The periodical has been _____ in CNKI. net and hopefully, will be _____ by CPCI-SSH (ISTP) soon.

Taking paper quality and topic relevance as the only criterion for publication, the periodical is _____ papers on an ongoing and year-round basis, specifically, on the following _____:

- Business translation theories, practices, and teaching
- Inquiries and insights into translation industry
- Reviews on translation works, etc.

Your papers may be written in Chinese, English, Russian, Japanese, Korean, or Spanish, and it should contain the following elements and their corresponding English translations:

- _____, _____, _____ and _____
- _____, _____, _____
- Information about the author (_____, one paragraph)

Your submission should be in .doc format, no less than 3 pages; accepted manuscripts are typed with 1.5 spacing and with a font point size of 12 (as submitted in Microsoft Word format); and the reference should follow the APA style, i.e. American Psychological Association (APA) Format (6th Edition, 2009). Since any submissions to the periodical will be submitted to _____, it is highly recommended to list such _____ as the article title, author name, degree, title, and _____, and _____ only on a separate page.

If your submission is _____ in our periodical, it shall not be published in any periodical(s) elsewhere without the _____ of the Editorial Office of *Business Translation*. Please remember that the Editorial Office _____ to refuse submitted work. Therefore, you may be asked to remove extreme graphic material or excessive language, unless otherwise _____. Your submission would be at your own _____ and not be returned in case of no _____ within the _____ of 5 weeks upon receiving it.

Editorial Office (China):

E-mail: sibt_j@163.com; 123388728@qq.com Tel:0411-84710460; 15640288993

Add:315, Shixuezhai, No.217 Jianshan Street, Dalian

Lesson 2
Conference Correspondence

Overview

☑ Reading

- Conference correspondence: Style a content
- Inquiry letters
- Reviewers' decision letters

☑ Vocabulary

- Academic words: Conference correspondence

Reading

❶ Discuss the following questions with your partner.

1. Have you ever exchanged letters with the organizers of a conference? If yes, for what purposes?
2. What are normally the purposes of establishing correspondences with the organizers of a conference?
3. Whom do conference participants correspond with to make inquiries or requests?
4. What are the frequently used ways of conference correspondences?
5. What is the style of conference correspondence letters? And why do you think so?

❷ Read the paragraphs and check your answers.

> To be an effective conference communicator, you should be, first of all, familiar with conference correspondence. Pre- or post-conference correspondence may vary greatly in terms of content, but do not go beyond the scope of making inquiries, explaining reasons, specifying requests, seeking possibilities, etc. Generally speaking, for routines and conference information, the possible contact persons are usually the secretary-general, the chairperson, the designated contact person, and the like.
>
> There are many ways of conference correspondence, such as phone calls, letters and emails. Among them, letters still remain the most frequently used means of conference correspondence whether by post or email. Letters and emails involved in conference correspondence are a kind of formal writing.

❸ Discuss with your partner and tell whether the following 7 parts are included in a formal letter. If yes, identify them in the given sample letter.

1. The heading	5. The complimentary close
2. The inside address	6. The signature
3. The salutation	7. The envelope
4. The body	

English Department
Beijing Foreign Language Univ.
Beijing, 100081
Sept. 5, 1997

Editor
Newsweek International
444 Madison Avenue
New York, NY 100022
USA

Dear Editor,

  I read in *Newsweek* that updated second edition of the unabridged Random House *Dictionary of the English Language* is being published. I would be very grateful if you could give me some information on where and how I can get a copy of the dictionary and if there is a less expensive edition than the one described.

  Thank you for any help you can give me.

Yours sincerely,
Xue Shu

Please note down the key points of formal letter writing:

Basic parts of a formal letter:
_____
_____

Location of different parts:
_____
_____

Regular expressions in a formal letter:
_____
_____
_____
_____

❹ **Read the sample inquiry letters and answer the following questions.**

> **Sample 1**
>
> Dear Editors,
>
>   I am WANG Lei, the postgraduate student of Tianjin Polytechnic University, P. R. China. I dispatched my manuscript to your journal on May 3rd 2015, but have not yet received acknowledgement of their safe arrival. I fear that it may have been lost and should be grateful if you would let me know whether or not you have received it. If not, I will send my manuscript again. Thank you in advance for your help.
>
>   Yours sincerely,
>
>   WANG Lei

1. What is the purpose of the letter?

2. What are the main parts of the letter?

3. Is this letter formal or informal? Why do you think so?

> **Sample 2**
>
> Dear Professor Smith,
>
>   I am WANG Lei, the postgraduate student of Tianjin Polytechnic University, P. R. China. It has been more than two months since I submitted my paper (No: 36572) for possible presentation and publication. I have not yet received a reply and am wondering whether you have reached a decision. I would appreciate if you could let me know what you have decided as soon as possible. Thank you.
>
>   Sincerely yours,
>
>   WANG Lei

1. What is the purpose of the letter?

2. What are the main parts of the letter?

3. If you need to write a letter to ask for permission of 1-day delay of paper submission, how will you arrange for the framework of your letter?

> **Tips:**
> Conference correspondences are relatively formal in style, which means they are objective, direct, courteous, and relatively impersonal. The wording should be exact and concise.
>
> Normally, when sending a letter to the conference organizing committee to make inquiries or requests, the writer/author will include the following content in his/her letter:
> - Who "I" am and why "I" write this letter;
> - What information or favor "I" expect to obtain;
> - Expressing gratitude to the letter receiver.

❺ Read the sample letters of reply and answer the following questions.

> **Sample 3**
> Dear Dr. Wang,
> Thank you for submitting your work to *Materials Letters*.
> Before we pass on manuscripts to the Journal Editor, who is responsible for the scientific assessment, we perform an initial check against formal technical criteria (structure of submission, adherence to the guide for authors and English language usage).
> We regret to inform you that your manuscript has failed in the initial formal technical criteria assessment.
> (1) USE OF ENGLISH
> In its current state, the level of English throughout your manuscript does not meet the journal's required standard. Authors have the responsibility to present papers in good English which can be understood by the journal's readership. If reviewers cannot understand your work as easily as possible, the acceptability of your article will be lowered greatly.
> We will NOT consider a revised version of your manuscript, unless it has received a complete re-writing to improve the level of English.
> (2) STRUCTURE AND COMPLETENESS
> Your manuscript is NOT in accordance with every aspect listed within the author guidelines. Your manuscript should include, but not be limited to, the comments mentioned below.
> Language:
> - In its current state, the level of English throughout your manuscript does not meet the journal's desired standard. Please check the manuscript and refine the language carefully.
>
> Technical:
> - A minimum of two of the keywords is to be chosen from the list of fixed keywords that can be found at the end of the guide for authors.
> - The maximum number of illustrations is strictly limited to five. If the maximum of 5 illustrations is used, then the total number of words must be reduced to 1,600.

(3) FINAL WORD

If you thoroughly revise your manuscript in accordance with what is stated above in (1) and (2) we welcome you to resubmit it, however, we will again check your manuscript for adherence to technical criteria. Passing this is not a guarantee that your submission will subsequently proceed to the peer review process, which is a decision to be made at the sole discretion of the Editor.

PLEASE NOTE: *Materials Letters* would like to enrich online articles by displaying interactive figures that help the reader to visualize and explore your research results. For this purpose, we would like to invite you to upload figures in the MATLAB .FIG file format as supplementary material to our online submission system. Elsevier will generate interactive figures from these files and include them with the online article on SciVerseScienceDirect. If you wish, you can submit .FIG files along with your revised submission.

Yours sincerely,
Materials Letters

1. Who is the letter writer? What is the writer in charge of?

   _____

   _____

2. What is the journal's decision? In which tone does the letter writer inform the journal's decision to the author? Can you find any evidence in the text?

   _____

   _____

   _____

3. What should the author do next?

   _____

Sample 4

Dear Dr. Wang,

I have now received and considered the reviews of your revised manuscript submitted to *Academy of Management Review* "HUMAN RESOURCE SYSTEMS AND HELPING IN ORGANIZATIONS: A RELATIONAL PERSPECTIVE" (Manuscript AMR-09-0402. R1). All three of your reviewers agree that your manuscript has made good progress and you've made a good effort to respond to their earlier concerns. We all appreciate the clearer focus on the linkages between HR systems and helping and recognize the time and energies you put into this revision.

Your reviewers also agree that at this stage, several issues remain. I share the opinion that your revised manuscript is much improved and that you undertook great effort to be responsive to the earlier feedback. And, while I agree there are still some issues to address, I believe these issues can be addressed with relatively moderate additional effort and thus, I am pleased to **conditionally accept your manuscript for publication in AMR** subject to the changes below. Congratulations! I will not be returning your revised manuscript to the reviewers, but instead will be ensuring the remaining changes are made on their behalf.

In terms of the remaining changes I'd like you to make, it is important that you consider all the comments made by the reviewers but I would like to highlight the primary factors that I believe are necessary to move forward. I would like you to focus your energies on the points I note below.

...

Sincerely,
Dr. Jack Smith
Editor, *Academy of Management Review*

1. Who is the letter writer? Is he a reviewer of the paper mentioned?

2. What is the journal's final decision? In which tone does the letter writer inform the journal's decision to the author? Can you find some evidence in the text?

3. What should the author do next?

Tips:

The letter of reply from the editor, which informs the author of the paper acceptance, usually consists of the following parts:
- Why "I" write the letter—to inform the author of the paper acceptance;
- What "you" should do next—to make further modifications according to the feedback of the reviewers; (sometimes the reviewers' comments are directly attached hereafter, but sometimes not attached)
- Expressing gratitude and best wishes briefly to the letter receiver. (This part is omitted sometimes by some journals.)

In case of the paper rejection, the letter of reply from the editor is usually very brief, consisting of:
- Why "I" write the letter—to inform the author of the paper rejection;
- Why the paper is rejected—to show the author the evidences of failure to meet the assessment criteria; (this part is in fact very helpful to the author, but unfortunately, is omitted by some journals sometimes.)
- Expressing gratitude and best wishes briefly to the letter receiver. (This part is omitted sometimes by some journals.)

Vocabulary

❶ Discuss with your partner and find more routine expressions in conference correspondence letters.

> **To address the letter receiver:**
> Dear Sir or Madam, Dear Professor Smith, Dear Dr. White
> _____
> _____
>
> **To state the reasons for writing the letter:**
> It has been more than 1 month since I submitted my paper …
> I have not received acknowledgement of their safe arrival …
> _____
> _____
>
> **To express gratitude:**
> Thank you.
> I have been grateful to …
> Your effort is highly appreciated …
> _____
> _____
>
> **To make request/inquiry**
> I wonder if you could …
> Could you please kindly send me …?
> It would be much appreciated if …
> _____
> _____

❷ Translate the following sentences into English or Chinese.

1. 很荣幸受邀参加这次学术盛会。

2. 我因生病，未能按时提交论文摘要。请问现在能否补交？如何补交？

3. 不知文章是否收到，烦请告知。

4. 盼尽早告知论文能否被贵刊录用,谢谢。

5. Your manuscript entitled "XXXX" has been accepted for publication in *Computer Science*.

6. One of the more significant concerns that remain for the reviewers and myself relates to the propositions in your manuscript.

7. The reviewers pointed out several instances where some additional clarification would be very helpful to the reader.

8. Reviewer 3 suggests that you consider several additional points for your discussion section.

❸ **Write letters according to the situations given below.**
1. Bill Jannotta, a research fellow in the Chinese Academy of Sciences, has learned from *Progress in Physics* that the International Conference on Thermodynamics will be held in Sydney. So he writes to request for details of the conference announcement, invitations and other relevant information.

2. You have received a reply from the editor, which is listed below. Please write a reply to the editor.

Dear Dr. Wang,

　　Thank your for submitting your revised manuscript to the designated reviewers. I have now received three reviews of your resubmission. Although the reviewers appreciated your thorough revision, they raised a few more methodological concerns that should be clarified or discussed before acceptance. None of the comments should be too difficult to deal with although I do hope you will put some serious thought into these methodological issues. If you could please revise your manuscript within the next 3-4 weeks and return it with a detailed reply to each of the reviewer comments, I am hopeful it will not require further peer review.

　　...

Sincerely,
Dr. Mike Brown
Editor, <i>Journal of Management</i>

Appendixes

Appendix 1 Common citation styles

Citation styles		Disciplines
IEEE (Institute of Electrical and Electronics Engineers)		*Engineering, IT*
MLA (Modern Language Association)		*Humanities*
APA (American Psychological Association)		*Psychology, education, social sciences*
ACS (American Chemical Society)		*Chemistry*
Chicago (The Chicago Manual of Style)	Chicago A	*History, humanities*
	Chicago B	*Sciences, social sciences, humanities*
Harvard (Harvard Referencing Style)		*Economics*
ICMJE (International Committee of Medical Journal Editors)		*Medicine*
NLM (National Library of Medicine)		*Medicine*
Vancouver (Vancouver Style)		*Medicine*
AMA style (American Medical Association)		*Medicine*
OSCOLA (OSCOLA Referencing)		*Law*
CBE (Council of Biology Editors)		*Biology*
AIP (American Institute of Physics)		*Physics*
USGS (the United States Geological Survey)		*Geology*

Appendix 2 Academic Word List

The Academic Word List (AWL) is a word list released in 2000 by Averil Coxhead at Victoria University of Wellington, New Zealand. The AWL has 570 word families. They were selected from a corpus of millions of words from over 400 academic texts, which came from 28 academic subject areas within the disciplines of Arts, Commerce, Law and Science. The AWL covers 10% of words in academic texts. Since the words in the AWL are not connected with any particular subject, they are useful for all students. The list of these 570 words was further divided into ten sublists. The sublists and relevant worksheets are available on the following websites:

http://www.englishvocabularyexercises.com/academic-word-list/index.html
https://academic-englishuk.com/wp-content/uploads/2021/02/Academic-Word-List-AWL.pdf
https://www.ieltsbuddy.com/awl-exercises.html

A

abandon	abstract	academic	access
accommodation	accompanied	accumulation	accurate
achieve	acknowledged	acquisition	adaptation
adequate	adjacent	adjustment	administration
adult	advocate	affect	aggregate
aid	albeit	allocation	alter
alternative	ambiguous	amendment	analogous
analysis	annual	anticipated	apparent
appendix	appreciation	approach	appropriate
approximated	arbitrary	area	aspects
assembly	assessment	assigned	assistance
assume	assurance	attached	attained
attitude	attributed	author	authority
automatically	available	aware	

B

behalf	benefit	bias	bond
brief	bulk		

C

capable	capacity	category	cease
challenge	channel	chapter	chart
chemical	circumstance	cited	civil
clarity	classical	clause	code
coherence	coincide	collapse	colleague
commenced	comment	commission	commitment
commodity	communication	community	compensation
compiled	complement	complex	component
compound	comprehensive	comprise	computer
conceived	concentration	concept	conclusion
concurrent	conduct	conference	confined
confirmed	conflict	conformity	consent
consequence	considerable	consistent	constant
constitutional	constraint	construction	consultation
consumer	contact	contemporary	context
contract	contradiction	contrary	contrast
contribution	controversy	convention	conversely
converted	convinced	cooperative	coordination
core	corporate	corresponding	couple
create	credit	criteria	crucial
cultural	currency	cycle	

D

data	debate	decade	decline
deduction	definite	definition	demonstrate
denote	deny	depression	derived
design	despite	detected	deviation
device	devoted	differentiation	dimension
diminish	discretion	discrimination	displacement
display	disposal	distinction	distortion
distribution	diversity	document	domain
domestic	dominant	draft	dramatic
duration	dynamic		

E

economic	edition	element	eliminate
emerged	emphasis	empirical	enable
encounter	energy	enforcement	enhanced
enormous	ensure	entity	environment
equation	equipment	equivalent	erosion
error	establish	estate	estimate
ethical	ethnic	evaluation	eventually
evidence	evolution	exceed	excluded
exhibit	expansion	expert	explicit
exploitation	export	exposure	external
extract			

F

facilitate	factor	feature	federal
fee	file	final	financial
finite	flexibility	fluctuation	focus
format	formula	forthcoming	foundation
founded	framework	function	fundamental
fund	furthermore		

G

gender	generated	generation	global
goal	grade	granted	guarantee
guideline			

H

hence	hierarchical	highlighted	hypothesis

I

identical	identified	ideology	ignored
illustrated	image	immigration	impact
implementation	implication	implicit	imply
imposed	incentive	incidence	inclination
income	incompatible	incorporated	index

indicate
inferred
initial
input
instance
integration
interaction
interval
investment
issue

individual
infrastructure
initiative
insert
institute
integrity
intermediate
intervention
invoked
item

induced
inherent
injury
insight
instruction
intelligence
internal
intrinsic
involved

inevitably
inhibition
innovation
inspection
integral
intensity
interpretation
investigation
isolated

J

job

journal

justification

L

label
legal
license
logic

labor
legislation
likewise

layer
levy
link

lecture
liberal
location

M

maintenance
marginal
media
mental
minimal
minority
motivation

major
mature
mediation
method
minimized
mode
mutual

manipulation
maximum
medical
migration
minimum
modified

manual
mechanism
medium
military
ministry
monitoring

N

negative
nonetheless
notwithstanding

network
normal
nuclear

neutral
norms

nevertheless
notion

O

objective

obtained

obvious

occupational

occur	odd	offset	ongoing
option	orientation	outcomes	output
overall	overlap	overseas	

P

panel	paradigm	paragraph	parallel
parameter	participation	partnership	passive
perceive	percent	period	persistent
perspective	phase	phenomenon	philosophy
physical	plus	policy	portion
posed	positive	potential	practitioner
preceding	precise	predicted	predominantly
preliminary	presumption	previous	primary
prime	principal	principle	prior
priority	procedure	process	professional
prohibit	project	promote	proportion
prospect	protocol	psychology	publication
publish	purchase	pursue	

Q

qualitative	quotation

R

radical	random	range	ratio
rational	reaction	recovery	refine
regime	region	registered	regulation
reinforce	rejected	relaxed	release
relevant	reliance	reluctant	removed
required	research	resident	resolution
resource	response	restore	restraint
restricted	retained	revealed	revenue
reverse	revision	revolution	rigid
role	route		

S

scenario	schedule	scheme	scope

section	sector	security	select
sequence	series	sex	shift
significant	similar	simulation	site
so-called	solely	somewhat	sought
source	specific	specified	sphere
stability	statistics	status	straightforward
strategy	stress	structure	style
submit	subordinate	subsequent	subsidiary
substitution	successive	sufficient	sum
summary	supplementary	survey	survive
suspend	sustainable	symbolic	

T

tape	target	task	team
technical	technique	technology	temporary
tension	termination	text	theme
theory	thereby	thesis	topic
trace	traditional	transfer	transformation
transition	transmission	transport	trend
trigger			

U

ultimately	undergo	underlying	undertaken
unified	uniform	unique	utility

V

validity	variable	vehicle	version
via	violation	virtually	visible
vision	visual	volume	voluntary

W

welfare	whereas	whereby	widespread

References

1. https://www.thebookdesigner.com/2009/10/self-publishing-basics-the-copyright-page/
2. https://www.diggypod.com/images/long-copyright-page.png
3. https://kindlepreneur.com/book-copyright-page-examples-ebook/
4. https://www.vocabulary.com/lists/218701
5. https://www.englishclub.com/grammar/sentence/sentence-structure.htm
6. http://www.englishlanguageguide.com/grammar/subject.asp
7. https://www2.bc.edu/robert-stanton/en133/essay%20conventions.html
8. http://publiclibrariesonline.org/2015/10/why-libraries-win-library-lending-vs-e-book-subscription-services/
9. https://www.businesswire.com/news/home/20180103005624/en/APAC-Tops-Global-RTD-Tea-Coffee-Market
10. http://www.everythingenglishblog.com/?p=474
11. http://www.chinadaily.com.cn/a/201908/01/WS5d4250b9a310d8305640231c.html
12. https://en.dpm.org.cn/exhibitions/current/2018-07-12/2822.html
13. http://www.chinadaily.com.cn/a/201909/04/WS5d6f4fa3a310cf3e35569aa9.html
14. https://en.dpm.org.cn/exhibitions/current/2018-07-12/2822.html
15. https://www.apa.org/index
16. https://style.mla.org/
17. https://www.chicagomanualofstyle.org/tools_citationguide.html

18. https://www.thoughtco.com/style-guide-reference-work-1691998
19. https://www.writingforward.com/writing-resources/style-guides-essential-writing-resources Feb 22, 2018
20. https://apastyle.apa.org/manual/
21. https://dictionary.cambridge.org/us/dictionary/english/typology
22. https://www.eila.univ-paris-diderot.fr_mediauserchristopher_gledhillm1_cm3_field_tenor_mode_framework_gledhill.pdfid = userchristopher_gledhillm1_technical_
23. https://www.ldoceonline.com/
24. https://www.oxfordlearnersdictionaries.com/
25. https://dictionary.cambridge.org/
26. https://www.britannica.com/
27. https://www.englishclub.com/grammar/sentence/sentence-structure.htm
28. http://www.englishlanguageguide.com/grammar/subject.asp
29. https://science.sciencemag.org/content/373/6554/488 2021/8/9/10:00
30. https://www.thoughtco.com/narration-in-composition-and-speech-1691415
31. http://www.sciencemag.org/news/2018/08/your-dog-lying-other-dogs-about-its-size
32. https://targetstudy.com/languages/english/direct-and-indirect-speech.html
33. https://www.thoughtco.com/what-is-direct-speech-1690393
34. https://www.thoughtco.com/reported-speech-p2-1692045
35. McGuire, B. & Bemis, K. E. (2017). Scent marking in shelter dogs: Effects of body size. Appl. Anim. Behav. Sci. 186, 49–55.
36. https://www.tandfonline.com/doi/abs/10.1080/17404622.2017.1400679?journalCode = rcmt20
37. https://www.visionlearning.com/en/library/Process-of-Science/49/Description-in-Scientific-Research/151
38. https://en.dpm.org.cn/collections/collections/2015-05-27/3960.html
39. https://www.britannica.com
40. https://www.space.com/change-5-mission.html

41. https://www.sciencenewsforstudents.org/article/explainer-what-vaccine

42. https://www.worldhistory.org/Oracle_Bones/

43. http://www.softschools.com/examples/science/ionization_energy_examples/22/

44. https://www.rightshape.com/food-digestion-guide/

45. https://www.oxfordlearnersdictionaries.com/

46. https://dictionary.cambridge.org/us/dictionary/english/typology

47. https://mp.weixin.qq.com/s/vDT1OkhdHccksRl5g_GvUQ

48. https://www.theguardian.com/commentisfree/2018/aug/10/dna-ancestry-tests-cheap-data-price-companies-23andme

49. Cahill, J. (1978). *Parting at the Shore*. New York: Weatherhill.

50. Ochsner, T. (2019). *Rain or Shine: An Introduction to Soil Physical Properties and Processes*. Oklahoma: Oklahoma State University.

51. Nakano, M. (2020). *Red Seal Landscape Horticulturist Identify Plants and Plant Requirements*. Columbia: Kwantlen Polytechnic University.

52. Schmittner, A. (2017). *Introduction to Climate Science*. Oregan: Oregan State University.

53. Morley, J. (2015). *Academic Phrasebank*. Manchester: The University of Manchester.

54. Weissberg, R. & Buker, S. (1990). *Writing up Research*. New Jersey: Prentice Hall.

55. Giniger, S., Dispenzieri, A. & Eisenberg, J. (1983). Age, experience and performance on speed and skill jobs in an applied setting. *Journal of Applied Psychology*, 68, 472–73.

56. Bruce, I. (2008). *Academic Writing and Genre: A Systematic Analysis*. New York: Continuum.

57. 霍夫曼(Hofmann, A. H.). (2012). 科技写作与交流：期刊论文、基金申请书及会议演讲(美)[M]. 任胜利, 等译. 北京：科学出版社.

58. 李立光. (2012). 研究生英语阅读教程(提高级/第三版)[M]. 北京：中国人民大学出版社.